NEW BEST FRIENDS
Playground Strategies for Market Dominance

BY

PETER HUSAK

with

Grant D. McKenzie

ISBN-13: 978-1466436350
ISBN-10: 1466436352

To Mike Rhue -
The original New Best Friend

Table of Contents

Preface

Every day as my dad headed out the door for work, he would say, "Be nice to everybody." My sister and I would smile and take note as we ate our breakfast cereal and our mother made PB&Js for our lunch. Over time, this statement became so ingrained I felt I could be nice to all kinds of people.

In high school, I said "hi" to almost everyone in the hallways and made friends with the popular kids, as well as those who weren't so popular. I tried to understand the different and unique qualities people had and appreciate them for who they were, which got me involved in a lot of different activities.

When my dad brought me to work with him, I talked to his peers in the executive suite, but like him, I also enjoyed talking to the employees in the manufacturing shop. The Chicago area is full of different ethnicities and cultures, so I enjoyed talking to workers from Western Europe, Canada, Mexico, and even Eastern European Slavic countries. I grew to understand you have to communicate with all types of people to accomplish business goals. I also discovered no matter who you meet, a thread ties you to that person, and your goal is to find that thread. It might be where you grew up, your hobbies, your work, your likes or dislikes, but no matter what differences may exist, there is a thread that ties each of us to one another. If I could find those threads, crack a smile on their faces, and get them talking about themselves (which is something people love to do), I knew I was getting somewhere.

*****

I had an unusual childhood because I led a dual life. In the winter, I lived on the North Shore, the northern suburbs of Chicago, where I went to school, played hockey, and participated in many other sports. In the summer, I put on my boots and hat and headed west to ride horses and be a cowboy.

Sometimes, I feel sorry for my dad. "What a weird kid," he'd say. He was a Chicagoan and an avid boater, raising a kid who didn't want to sail or water ski, but who would rather ride a horse. He shook his head when he saw me wearing chaps and a cowboy hat and watching old western movies on TV, living in a Chicago suburb. I wasn't happy in Chicagoland, but I appreciated the education I received and the competitive edge developed in a large city.

Hockey also contributed to my competiveness. As a boy, we played hockey in the backyard on a frozen pond, in the neighboring parks, and within the town's hockey program. Hockey is a great game. It's fast and hard-hitting, but when played with finesse, it's an art. I still play for the love of the game. I tell my son he needs to be a gentlemen at home, around the community, and at school, but when he steps between the boards and onto the ice, he should become a terrible, red dragon, play with all the effort he can, and leave nothing on the ice—no regrets. I tell him to play so hard that afterward, in the locker room, he should be gasping for breath. When you do this, you will drive home with a smile on your face. This is the same feeling you should have with your business.

*****

My mother, who was born and raised near Chicago, went on many trips with my grandparents to Colorado and Wyoming, where she grew to believe the Rocky Mountains were the best place on earth. She loved it so much she decided to attend The Colorado College in the mid-1950's. After one year, though, she transferred to Northwestern University so she could be close to home again, but she never lost the awe for the mountains and the beauty of the western frontier.

The summer before my third grade year, my parents brought me to Estes Park, Colorado. They did something on our visit that changed my life forever; they introduced me to a sorrel gelding named "Red" and let me ride him. Once I got atop ol' Red, that was it! That was all I wanted to do. I was the Lone Ranger, John Wayne, and all the other cowboy heroes from the movies I'd seen. The cowboy life quickly became my passion. After that, I spent most of my summers in either Colorado or Wyoming, riding horses, working on ranches, and living the cowboy dream.

As a kid, my imagination about the West grew while looking up at the framed oil paintings and etchings hanging in my paternal grandmother's living room. Her brother, William Ellings Gollings, or Bill Gollings, was a western artist from Sheridan, Wyoming. Today, his paintings are extremely valuable at auction. Like me, he traveled west from Chicago to be a cowboy, but he did it in the late 1800's, when the Wild West was still wild. Bill was a cowboy, a horseman, and an avid archer, as well as an important artist. He lived in the West when the stagecoach was still running and cowboys herded cattle before the fences. He was also a friend to the Native American.

In Bill's time, the cowboy lived by a code, a code of the West. I believe many in the West still live by that code. We honor our relationships, we back our friends up, no matter what, and we help our friends when they need it.

*****

The day after high school graduation, I packed up my 1966 Ford F250 step-side pickup, with a Professional Rodeo Cowboys Association sticker on the back bumper, and headed for Colorado Springs with everything I owned and never looked back. I attended The Colorado College, where I was inspired to love to learn and developed a deeper passion for the West. In September of my senior year, my father sat me down and said, "You need to interview for jobs this year while you finish college. Your mother and I will come out for your graduation. We will stay at the Antlers Hotel; you can stay with us, if you like. After you receive your diploma, we will take you out to lunch and maybe even dinner. You can stay with us at the hotel that night if you wish. The next morning I am going to hand you a hundred dollar bill and we are done!" I appreciated my Dad giving me plenty of notice, so I did interview like a mad man my senior year at CC. A few potential employers tried to get me to move away from the West, but I was not interested.

The West is a place where you can still feel free. The West still has wide-open spaces, people are still friendly, the entrepreneurs are still gun-slinging cowboys, and the frontier is still alive. My unique upbringing allows me to communicate with fast-talking, big city people from the Midwest, slow-talking, tobacco-chewing cowboys from the high prairie, and everything in between. Through my experience, I learned I was much more "attractive" in the saddle than in penny loafers.

Being in the saddle reveals who I truly am. I've found a home in Colorado Springs because I can ride my horse, legally, down Main Street (during the Pikes Peak or Bust Rodeo Street Breakfast) and it's considered a normal thing. I call this blend of business and pleasure "blurring," because you are blurring the lines separating many people from their true selves. When I am riding down the trail with a customer talking business am I working or am I having fun? The answer is "both."

I believe each of us has individual, special, God-given qualities only we possess that, when harnessed, can influence the community and even the world. I believe my job as leader of a company is to hire people with great qualities and then harness their gifts so they may shine. This is, in fact, the Purpose of OfficeScapes, Colorado Springs.

*****

I learned how to select a Purpose and Core Values from Verne Harnish, a well-known consultant and author of *Mastering the Rockefeller Habits*. In the early years of OfficeScapes, before he became wildly successful and famous, we hired Verne as our facilitator and consultant. He taught us the boring, dry, and less-meaningful mission statements of the past were not as effective as the Purpose and Core Values of his system. He said the Purpose of a company should come from the founder and CEO. Why did the CEO start the company? What drives the CEO to succeed in a business? After the CEO sets the Purpose, the executive team works to develop a set of Core Values. Verne asked, if we sent our best employees to Mars to represent OfficeScapes, who would we send and why. We selected the best people and defined why we selected them, based on the qualities they possessed. We captured, sorted, defined, and questioned these qualities until we had a set of Core Values describing who we were.

This set of Core Values defines our company personality, who we strive to be, and our culture. We use this set of Core Values to hire people and, quite frankly, fire people, because if people's values and ethics don't line up with our Core Values, they shouldn't work at OfficeScapes. The OfficeScapes Colorado Springs Core Values are:

- Deliver "WOW" through innovative excellence.
- Do the right thing.
- Whatever it takes.
- We figure it out.
- Deal direct and say it straight.
- Shine in the community.

These Core Values and Purpose sit on the top of a planning pyramid that drives our business plan, which cascades from a 3-5 year plan, a one-year plan, quarterly plan, monthly plan, and weekly plan. This Gazelle's system from Verne Harnish has been our successful system for over 14 years.

Our business success has been a journey. We recently went to Zappos.com in Las Vegas to learn their business practices, see their culture in action, and understand their passion for the customer. Since going to Zappos, we've tried to continue defining our culture. In one company meeting exercise, we tackled the definition of the Core Values further so each person really understood who we are as a company. I am proud to say one of the consistent answers describing OfficeScapes is "family." The players on 1980 US Olympic men's hockey team, coached by Herb Brooks, gave this same answer about their team, one of the most cohesive and well-developed teams in history. When I heard that answer, I knew we were getting somewhere, just as Herb Brooks did.

*****

I wrote this book because I wanted to tell my kids what I was good at - what my gift was. I read my grandfather's short memoir years ago and the itch to write something similar always lingered. If no one else reads this book, at least my kids will know one of the major gifts their dad had. Making New Best Friends.

Introduction

The time for extracting a lesson from history is ever at hand for those who are wise.

—Demosthenes

Johnny is a highly successful businessman. When he received his Small Businessperson of the Year Award, dozens of his closest friends filled the room, cheering his accomplishments. He won the award for doubling his company's sales and driving ten of his competitors out of business since becoming CEO. He streamlined his company's processes, found more and more ways to "wow" his customers, and made significant contributions to the community.

1

To Johnny, though, all of that was merely "running the business." He credited his success to the network of friends he'd created over that time. Through these relationships, he was able to make a difference in the lives of his employees, his customers, and in those throughout the community. For Johnny, that's what success should be about.

The award citation and nomination letters echoed Johnny's sentiments toward his network. They said Johnny creates relationships in the community that lead to teaming on the jobsite and makes it a point to meet and become friends with every company representative working with him on any particular job. Everything is a team effort with Johnny and the people within his network.

One nominator said each new contact becomes a "new best friend" and that Johnny nurtures those relationships until they really are his best friends. That was no surprise to Johnny, who treats every new contact as he did his friends when he was young. The lessons he learned building and maintaining relationships when he was on the playground have become just as useful and just as relevant in the boardroom.

Creating a network of new best friends will lead to success for you and your business, just like it did for Johnny and for me.

Back to Basics

When you were young, you had a group of friends you did things with, but you also had that special group of "best friends." Those were the ones you trusted with your most valuable possessions. You trusted them to be looking out for your interests just as you were looking out for theirs. You never expected anything from them; you just knew they'd be there when you needed them.

What would it be like to have a business network built entirely of best friends? These "new best friends" (NBFs) would call you unexpectedly with new tips. They'd always think of you before passing information to someone else. They'd give you information without asking for anything in return. When you were trying to win a contract or close a sale, they'd support you and help in the background, putting in a good word with your customer or helping you put your best foot forward. If you had a network of new best friends, not only would business be more profitable, it would be fun.

Fun at OfficeScapes

A good friend and mentor, Mike Rhue, once told me I should always be looking for a new best friend. He meant that sincerely because he recognized the importance of strong personal relationships within a business network. He knew a network of NBFs was far more powerful than a network of casual contacts.

"New best friend" became a code word between us, a lot like codes and secret languages many kids make up and share with their best friends. When Mike sent a "new best friend" over to me, I immediately knew two things about that person. First, I knew that person likely had information valuable to my business. Second, I knew Mike was taking a risk by introducing us. Even if the relationship didn't pan out, I still had a personal obligation to make Mike look good. That's what best friends do for each other.

Mike also taught me people are more likely to open up to you if they trust you, first. They will also be more likely to give out information if they are not worried about being overheard. As a result, the best way to get information and generate leads is with a personal, one-to-one relationship.

Business - War

No matter what business you're in, at the end of the day it's all about the relationships you create, build up, and nurture. I like to think of my NBF relationships as "strategic alliances," because I look at business as a form of warfare. In war, it's best to have a strong set of best friends by your side, not a group of casual contacts who will inevitably put their self-interests ahead of yours.

I earned a degree in history from The Colorado College. I was, and still am, fascinated by the rise and fall, mistakes and triumphs, and lessons taught by history's leaders and great thinkers. Philosophers, leaders, and strategists like Machiavelli, Sun Tzu, Peter the Great, Teddy Roosevelt, and Winston Churchill have all had a tremendous impact on the way I view the world of business. Machiavelli wrote, "Whoever wishes to foresee the future must first consult the past."

One of the many lessons I've learned from history is you must be a fighter to succeed. During the Civil War, Abraham Lincoln tried again and again to find a "fighting" general. When he finally placed Ulysses S. Grant in charge of the Union Army, the war ended in victory for the Union. Sun Tzu teaches the importance of the offensive and the comparative weakness of the defense. Winton Churchill's "never surrender" speech rallied a nation.

In business, the "enemy" is the competition. In 14 years at OfficeScapes, we were responsible for driving ten competitors out of business. Now, we are five times larger than our nearest competitor. We did it by targeting each competing company in turn for closing. I would rally our employees by taking them "en masse" in a rented bus to the competitor's home office and park in their parking lot. I'd give them what military commanders call an "order of battle," but instead of numbers of tanks, infantry, and artillery, I gave them numbers of employees, major product lines, major customers, and major partners. If the company had been treating its customers unethically, I told them that, as well. This made my "troops" hungry for the kill.

But that was just the beginning. By enlisting the aid of our strategic alliances (our NBFs), victory came easily. England fought hard and fought well throughout the Battle of Britain during World War II, but when the full weight of their strategic alliances came into play, "winning" turned into "defeating."

Hunters and Farmers

Being a fighter in business is a lot like being a hunter. It's an active mentality, going out to find new deals, capturing them, bringing them back to the office for everyone to enjoy, and then going back out again. For small- to medium-sized businesses to thrive, hunters must be in charge. Your friends must also be able to contribute to the hunt. They should know where the deal is, where to find the weak spot to attack, or what tools or "weapons" you'll need to bring it home. The information they offer needs to be actionable. In later chapters, I'll discuss how to find the right kind of NBFs for your business.

More often than not, farmers operate larger businesses, especially at the middle management levels. A farmer nurtures his field, waits for the rain, and has workers to help bring in the crop. In the same way, farmers in business nurture their existing accounts, reaping what they yield over time. This book is not for farmers, so unless you are prepared to go out, track down, and capture every deal, simply set the book down and return to your field.

History Speaks

The aftermath of the Battle of Gettysburg wonderfully illustrates the difference between hunters and farmers and the importance of being a hunter. Lincoln had been searching for a "fighting" general and thought he'd found one in George Meade. Meade's Army of the Potomac had just defeated Robert E. Lee's Army of Northern Virginia and sent them running toward the Potomac River. Lee's army trapped itself against the river, and Meade was poised to annihilate it and end the war.

Meade, however, was a "farmer." Rather than chase Lee down, he held back, trying to nurture his army by letting them recover from their difficult work at Gettysburg. Abraham Lincoln, who had just appointed Meade after firing General Joseph Hooker, expected Meade to fight. Lincoln was a hunter, and his response to Meade's hesitation showed his fighting spirit. He wrote, "As it is, the war will be prolonged indefinitely…Your golden opportunity is going and I am distressed immensely because of it."

Lincoln was a student of history. He once said, "Fellow citizens, we cannot escape history." He knew others had important things to say and kept an open mind with respect to the past.

Meade, on the other hand, thought the past had no lessons worth learning. He said, "I do not believe the truth will ever be known, and I have a great contempt for history."

In this book, we will look into the past and learn the lessons it has to teach. In particular, we will look into our own pasts and rediscover how we can use those lessons to make our business networks successful.

Johnny and Mary

Throughout this book, the lives of Johnny and Mary will illustrate the lessons we all learned as kids. While Johnny and Mary are fictional characters, the events in their lives reflect the lives of real people interviewed for this book. You may, therefore, find some part of your childhood—your past— reflected in theirs. In each chapter, you will see how the rules used to make friends as a kid become the rules to make your NBFs and how OfficeScapes applied those rules to go from market impotence to market dominance.

CHAPTER ONE

"Excellence in All We Do"

*The test of the artist does not lie
in the will with which he goes to
work, but in the excellence of the
work he produces.*

—Thomas Aquinas

When you were in school, those who were best at
something always drew more attention and more friends. The
star quarterback, the head cheerleader, and the valedictorian
always had a certain group of people who wanted to be around
them. In business, if you want to draw partners, customers, or
clients, you have to be the best at what you do.

I sit on the Board of Directors of the Pikes Peak or Bust Rodeo, which helps support military charities. In my interactions with the military, I've come to appreciate that, for them, mediocrity is a death sentence. Military members must always strive to be the best at what they do. In the U.S. Air Force, in particular, excellence is not so much a goal to achieve as it is a way of simply doing business. Their core values include the statement, "Excellence in all we do." For them, excellence is not a target. Excellence is the path that takes them where they want to be.

John Maxwell teaches that people attract others who are like themselves. His "Law of Magnetism[1]" states, "Who you are is who you attract." It means you will only attract strong, successful people if you are strong and successful yourself. Mediocrity, on the other hand, can only attract mediocrity. If you want to build a solid business network, you have to attract people who can help make it so. To do that, you must be the best you can possibly be.

---

[1] Maxwell, John C., *The 21 Irrefutable Laws of Leadership*, 1998, Maxwell Motivation, Inc.

Rule 1

Acquaintances are easy to attract, but attracting friends takes work.

Johnny stood nervously in front of his new fourth-grade class. His family had just moved to a new town, and he had to figure out how to fit in at this new school. This school was bigger than his last, and all the faces blurred together as he looked out over the crowded classroom. Johnny's mother gave him some good advice:

- *Be confident and stand tall.*
- *Introduce yourself.*
- *Smile as if you are enjoying yourself, even if you're not.*

Johnny took her advice, and people started interacting with him. They said "hi" in the hallways and asked questions about his old school. At first, Johnny accepted this as a good start, but he realized the other kids were still leaving him out of all the activities he wanted to join. When he tried to start activities of his own, no one followed. They were all committed to their own groups and didn't see anything new and appealing with Johnny.

Just doing what everyone else was doing wasn't enough for Johnny to be included. Simply knowing other kid's names and the type of activities they participated in wasn't a good enough relationship to be invited to participate. In order to break into one of these groups, someone had to notice him and invite him in.

*****

As a new sales associate, Johnny feels like he did in fourth grade. The pool of potential partners and customers is dizzying, and he doesn't really know where to begin. His management and some of his more experienced colleagues have given him some good advice:

- *Get on Facebook and advertise your profile.*
- *Get on Twitter and "tweet" your potential contacts.*
- *Set up a profile on LinkedIn and connect with LIONs[2].*
- *Find a leads group to join.*
- *Introduce yourself and have a business card ready.*
- *Smile as if you're enjoying yourself, even if you're not.*

---

[2] LinkedIn Open Networkers – people who have a very high number of connections and are willing to network with anyone, even if they've never met the person requesting the connection.

He's done all that, and more. Despite having literally millions of people connected to his LinkedIn profile, hundreds of friends on Facebook, and people following him on Twitter, he's still just another face in the crowd. The leads groups he attends are usually casual social gatherings, making him *literally* just another face in the crowd.

Being a face in the crowd wasn't enough for Johnny in fourth grade, and it isn't good enough for Johnny as an adult. He wants to get leads before the information "hits the streets," but to do so, he needs friends on the inside who are willing to invite him into their circles of friends.

*****

I learned early in my time at Xerox people were either "in the know" or they weren't. I wanted to talk to the ones who were. I could make cold calls, go to leads groups, and network with a variety of people, but in the end, I would end up with a pile of "acquaintances" and very few "friends."

I still do all the things everyone else does to network. I just don't rely on those methods for the success of my business. I've learned, through experience, I need to know about a new deal about six months before the information "hits the streets," and those leads rarely come from the more conventional resources.

I have been a part of one particular leads group locally for over 14 years. This group of 30+ businesspeople meets for presentations of "new" information, and the members receive a regular newsletter highlighting the latest information. With all that, I've only gotten two leads that amounted to anything for my business in the entire 14 years I've been with the group.

All these sources are easy to find and easy to use, but this is the "minor leagues" of networking. If you want to play in the big leagues in baseball, you must work hard, be noticed, and be called up. In big league networking, you must work hard, be noticed, and be invited into their inner circles.

Acquaintances are easy to attract, but it takes work to attract friends. So get ready to work.

RULE 2

Mediocrity attracts mediocrity.

Johnny tried to break into some playground groups through his many acquaintances, but with very little success. The kickball group chose him last, and although he was a good runner, he couldn't control his kick and couldn't make it to first base without being thrown out. The next day, the kickball group refused to let him back into the game.

Another time, Johnny tried to break into the group of boys who played basketball. He'd been learning hockey from his father since he was in preschool, and some of those skills helped him do well on the court, but he couldn't shoot the ball well. No matter how close he got to the basket, he could never score. The kids let him play if they needed an extra player, but they really didn't want him to play at all.

Through his experiences and through watching others, Johnny discovered the way to find a potential friend on the playground was to be good enough at something for others to notice you. Trying to force his way into the playground cliques wasn't working; someone had to invite him in. Everyone noticed the best basketball player, the best kickball player, or the best anything.

Johnny was probably the best in the school at hockey, but it was spring. No one could see him play. He had to excel at something the other kids could see. If the other kids couldn't see it, then he was just another face in the crowd.

*****

Johnny has built up a nice-sized business network using all the conventional methods. He's researched his contacts so he can speak intelligently when, or if, they ever meet face-to-face. He's approached some of them, but has usually received a cold shoulder when the topic turns to business. It's as though he was right back on the fourth-grade playground.

What Johnny fails to realize is his contacts are looking into him and his company the same way he's looking into theirs, and they don't see much that impresses them. Everything they find about Johnny and his company is only average or maybe slightly above. Nothing special. Nothing that would compel them to put forth any effort for him.

Johnny, however, knows he has something to offer his contacts, even though none of them, especially the ones who would be the most productive, will return his calls or answer his emails. Finally, he decides to treat these contacts the way he did the groups on the playground. He begins improving his reputation and, in the process, that of his company. He works toward the goal of having his company stand out from the rest and rise above the mediocre. As he begins to stand out, others see him and are drawn to him. If mediocrity attracts mediocrity, Johnny wants to repel it.

⁕⁕⁕⁕⁕

When I took over OfficeScapes, mediocrity was a way of life, for both the company and the industry in this region. Customers awarded contracts without regard to customer service. An outsider would have thought contracts were going to each company in turn. Customers only expected their furniture to arrive on time and intact.

Customer service was a foreign concept with the industry, so customers had very low expectations, and if customer service was a foreign concept, service after the sale was from another planet. Some companies even went so far as to be unethical in their treatment of their customers. They would leave essential materials or tasks out of their contract in order to get the low bid, and then add those materials or tasks back in after they'd won the contract. The best you could call any of the companies at that time, including OfficeScapes, was "average."

Shortly after taking over, I realized if any one of these dozen or so companies ever made an effort to be the best, if they ever set the goal of being #1 in the market and followed up on it, they could dominate the market. All the companies looked the same to the customers, but they would notice the company that made an effort to stand out.

Rule 3

When you stand out, customers,
clients, and partners will come to you.

Johnny noticed a group of boys in the large grassy section in the back of the playground, racing one another. Skating had made his legs strong, and his dad had taught him to run in the spring and summer to stay in shape. This was something at which he could excel. He practiced at home and, when he felt ready, he went to the group. When the fastest boy got set to race one of the other boys, Johnny set himself. Because he was some distance away from the group, some of the boys laughed at what he was doing.

When the starter shouted, "GO!" Johnny pushed off and ran the length of the course. He stopped at the other end and turned around to see the fastest boy (now the second fastest) just crossing the line. That kid had been the fastest since second grade and wasn't accustomed to losing. When he demanded a rematch, Johnny agreed and won, again.

Many other kids gathered for the rematch and saw Johnny's performance. The runners asked Johnny to stay in their group, and the boy he'd just beaten became his best friend. Other groups began asking Johnny to participate in their activities when he wasn't running.

Johnny didn't immediately become the center of attention on the playground. His excellence at running attracted those who could most benefit from his success and talent. Johnny knew he'd have to develop more skills if he wanted to be a part of other groups. His success might get him invited in, but a lack of skill would get him thrown out. It takes excellence to attract excellence, but a lack of excellence will repel it.

*****

Johnny, as a new sales professional, realizes very quickly he is one of many who are all doing the same things to win new contacts. No one really stands out from the crowd. Others are trying to force their way into relationships just as he did in the fourth grade. Unlike then, Johnny has no natural abilities to guide him. If he wants to excel, he has to put some work into it.

Johnny starts with his appearance. He goes out of his way to present an aura of professionalism and success that will be noticed in just about any crowded room. People in networking groups start introducing themselves to him more frequently, simply because he looks successful. They also notice him in meetings and other situations where he previously just blended into the background.

Johnny then changes his online presence. He creates new profiles he only uses for business so he can keep his social comments separate. He is also careful with what he posts on his personal profile, because customers can possibly see that information, as well. His total online presence is that of a successful, clean-cut businessman.

Johnny also changes the way he presents information to his customers. He spends extra time choosing fonts and creating formats that are crisp and eye-catching. For formal presentations, such as bids and proposals, he uses folders or report covers with his company's logo prominently displayed and always includes a business card. If his appearance can be noticed in a crowded room, his presentations should be noticed, too.

Making yourself and your work look good is only part of the battle, though. You can put on the best running shoes and an expensive tracksuit, but you still have to be able to run the race. Realizing this, Johnny studies everything his company has to offer. When anyone, especially a customer, has questions about the company, the most common reply from his peers and managers is, "Ask Johnny." He becomes the "go-to" guy, and soon people are requesting him by name for important meetings with bigger and bigger customers.

Mediocrity would never have drawn friends like his running buddies in school, and it will never bring the kind of customers he wants in business. The extra effort he puts into excellence more than pays for itself in the success it brings.

$$*****$$

One of the first things I changed at OfficeScapes was how we presented ourselves to our customers. Like Johnny, we began creating crisp, formatted documentation and presentations. Before I came to OfficeScapes, they presented typed bids written in language only the sales reps could understand. Once I took the reins, we had clearly-written, customer-focused bids and proposals. We divided them into sections and included an executive summary. We also used covers with our logo and always included business cards.

We changed the way we dressed, and even the way we behaved, in front of our customers. My rule was we should always dress just a little better than our customers did. I went so far as to have a "Dress for Success" class at our office to make my expectations clear. The image I wanted to put in front of a customer was a sales rep who was ready to close a multi-million dollar deal every minute of every day.

Some employees didn't like these new ideas or simply refused to abide by them. We fired about 30 people within a six-month period because they didn't have the same dedication to excellence as the rest of the company. I fired some for failing drug tests, while some didn't have to take the test for me to fire them—they were caught smoking pot in their cars in the parking lot. Some of the employees around that time spent more time in community corrections programs than at work. Others were stealing fiber-optic cable from job sites. In order to excel, we had to let go of all those who would hold us back.

At first, I took a lot of personal interest in the sales reps' business. I instituted tracking methods to keep informed about where our leads were going, but also to see who was doing their job and who was coasting. I implemented basic sales training and went with reps on sales calls to see how effective the training had been.

Once I saw the sales reps were doing well and our workforce was dedicated to shining within the industry, I started going out to make OfficeScapes shine within the community. That's when I entered the "major leagues" of networking and began attracting the connections that would help OfficeScapes grow even more than it already was.

In addition to all of these things, I restructured the business. If you remember, Johnny didn't have the skills necessary to be in both the running and the basketball groups. He had to choose one or the other, so he chose the one in which he had more talent. At that point, he had a choice of either forgetting about the basketball group or working hard to fit into it, as well.

At OfficeScapes, we had more skill and talent in contract work, but our company also had a retail division. I decided to keep up with the contract portion because it was our biggest revenue generator and had better long-term potential, not to mention the fact we were just better at contract work than retail. The original idea was a retail division would bring customers into the company and lead to larger contract orders down the line. I had to choose whether to abandon the retail division or dedicate more resources to bring it up to the same level as our contract business.

Ultimately, I decided to scrap the retail division and focus only on the contract business. The retail division would have taken many resources to bring it up to speed, and even then, it would never have produced notable results.

In our quest for excellence, we got rid of anything that would hold us back and polished whatever remained. Anything the customers would or could ever see was always top-notch. As a result, people began noticing OfficeScapes.

Summary

RULE 1: <u>Acquaintances are easy to attract, but attracting friends takes work.</u> It's easy to meet people and exchange business cards or add people to your online presence, but making friends who will be interested in the same things as you takes work. Building an NBF network isn't easy, but it's worth it.

RULE 2: <u>Mediocrity attracts mediocrity.</u> John Maxwell's Law of Magnetism says you will attract people who are the same as you. If you are mediocre, you will not attract the kind of friends who will help you become successful. You will remain nothing more than a face in a crowd.

RULE 3: <u>When you stand out, customers, clients, and partners will come to you.</u> Just as mediocrity attracts mediocrity, excellence attracts excellence. The first step to building a successful NBF network is to focus on excellence in yourself and in your company. When you're the best, people will come looking for you.

CHAPTER TWO

Finding Friends

"Friends have all things in common."
—Plato

Most kids learn the difference between having friends
and having acquaintances early in their lives. They may not be
able to articulate it, but they understand the difference between
knowing someone who takes a genuine interest in them and
just knowing someone. Once they reach this level of
understanding, they start down the path toward making new
best friends. By examining how these kids go about finding
new friends, you can better understand how to find NBFs for
your business network.

27

When building an NBF network, you should be more concerned with people than with what they have to offer. People do not live, work, or play inside business cards or social networking profiles. "Minor league" networks rely on tools like these to find connections. While these are valuable tools, you must be willing to go beyond the LinkedIn profile, Facebook page, and business cards you've collected at local networking group socials to play in the networking "major leagues." Relationships are created and nurtured through one-on-one interactions, and that's what separates professional networkers from the amateurs.

RULE 4

To be friends, you have to
have something in common.

One of the fastest ways to learn about people is to watch and listen. This came naturally to Mary because she was too introverted to jump into a group and start up a conversation. She stood near groups of girls and listened until someone inside the group invited her in. As she listened, she learned the girls separated themselves into cliques based on things they had in common. One group consisted of the gymnast/dancer girls who would later become cheerleaders. Another was made up of the brainy girls who would become doctors, lawyers, or engineers. Some girls belonged to several groups, such as the scholar-athletes who had something in common with both the brainy and the athletic girls.

As Mary learned about her classmates, she began to see she wouldn't be friends with the cheerleader group because she'd never taken–and never would, if she had any say in the matter–dance or gymnastics lessons. She would never join, or even want to join, many of the groups into which the girls divided themselves. On the other hand, some of the groups were very appealing.

Mary identified which girls were most likely to become friends with her based on the things they had in common. She had a lot in common with some of the brainy girls as well as some of the athletic girls. Her favorite playground game was tag, and one tight-knit group of girls always played tag during recess. All she had to do was work up the courage to talk to them. At first, she was a little unsure of how to approach a group of girls who were obviously such good friends already, but if she was ever going to make new friends, she would have to take the initiative.

*****

When Mary starts thinking about building an NBF network, she remembers making friends in elementary school. Back then, she became friends with girls with whom she had something in common. Now, as a businesswoman, she realizes she needs to concentrate on finding people who have something in common with both her and her business.

Mary is a business consultant working with companies across a broad spectrum of industries. Her network is vital to her business success. Her contacts within many of the companies she works with are training directors and human resources professionals, so anyone in a position like this would be a good NBF. Mary also does one-on-one training and consultation with the senior leadership of small- to medium-sized companies. One of the best ways to be introduced to these professionals is through their personal or administrative assistants. Because her clients typically pay her through their finance departments, an NBF who knows the company budget could also prove beneficial. Any of these people can give Mary actionable information about where to find a new deal or how to win it. Many more people can provide similar information, so Mary has more areas available in which she can find NBFs.

In order to build a large and successful network, she may have to get creative. She might, for example, approach people networked with her competitors. Sometimes, the best NBFs will come from unexpected places or unanticipated meetings. Like Mary, you must keep an open mind and be ready any time an NBF opportunity presents itself.

*****

When I started building the NBF network for OfficeScapes, I had to think about people who know about new office building construction or office building refurbishments early in the process. Commercial real estate brokers, architects, geotechnical engineers, and some general contractors are all people who will be working with our future customers. In fact, all of these will probably be working with the customer long before the customer has even begun to consider their office furniture needs in detail. Because we need to know about a new deal about six months before it's announced through the media outlets, these are just the people I want to bring into my network.

In a market the size of Colorado Springs, I need to network with all the architects, all the commercial real estate agents or brokers, all the commercial general contractors, and all the other people in all the other industries who feed my business. My friend and mentor, Mike Rhue, works in the much larger market of Denver, which has a population of about 2.5 million, compared to the 500,000 in Colorado Springs. In his market, he can afford to refine and narrow the criteria he wants in an NBF. It almost becomes a necessity. Either way, though, your NBFs must have something in common with your business.

Building an NBF relationship is about more than finding people who could be beneficial to your business, though. It's also about building a long-term personal relationship. In order to do this, you must blur the lines between business and pleasure. Early in my networking efforts, I joined the El Paso Club, a members-only social organization here in Colorado Springs. Not only did I get access to influential people in the community through my membership, I gained something I could offer others. It is now my favorite place to invite an NBF for a meal. The pleasure I get is having a fine meal in a quiet intimate atmosphere and the ability to give my NBFs who are not members a little something extra when I meet with them.

I am a cowboy, and anything dealing with the open spaces will draw my attention. That's why I joined the Pikes Peak Range Riders early in my network building, in addition to the El Paso Club. For me, the ultimate in blurring the lines between business and pleasure is being able to do business in the saddle, which happens with the Pikes Peak Range Riders. I have met about 300 NBFs between these two organizations, 20 of whom have contributed significantly to OfficeScapes' success.

Some people will recommend membership on a variety of community boards in order to open yourself up to more networking opportunities. If you join several boards expecting to get numerous good leads, though, you will likely be very disappointed. You'll spread yourself thin, feel overworked, and will most likely have neglected your business or fallen short on your commitments. When considering boards, you should apply the "blurring" concept. Find one board you can become passionate about and be dedicated to that board. I joined the Board of Directors for the Pikes Peak or Bust Rodeo due to my love and passion for the cowboy way. I'm a team roper and an auctioneer in my off time, so being on the board is a real treat for me. When people see that passion and dedication, they want to get to know me better, which gives me the opportunity to meet my next NBF. Another reason I am so passionate about this board is the Pikes Peak or Bust Rodeo supports military charities. Although I never served in the military, I am proud to honor those who do, whenever and however I can.

Rule 5

To meet new friends, you have
to know where to look.

Mary was shy and often intimidated by large groups of other kids. During recess, she sat under a tree in the corner of the playground, waiting for other kids to notice her. She talked with some of the girls who walked by, and they were friendly in return, but none of them ever stopped long enough to get to know her. She hoped one of the girls who played tag every day would walk by and talk to her. She tried talking to them between classes, but she was never able to introduce herself in all the bustle.

After a few days, Mary ventured out from under her tree and onto the playground. She joined in a soccer game and got to know the girls who played. She also spent time near the basketball court, and although the girls were nice to her, it wasn't what she wanted to do. She didn't have anything in common with the girls who played soccer and basketball. She hoped she could get to know the girls who played tag through the girls she was meeting everywhere else on the playground, but that never happened.

Finally, Mary worked up the courage to approach the part of the playground where the girls played tag. When she did, one of the girls recognized her from class and asked if she wanted to play. Surprised, Mary ran to join in. She realized if she'd just come there first, she'd have been making real friends much sooner.

*****

The lesson Mary learned in fourth grade repeated itself throughout her childhood and adolescence, so by the time she'd become a successful businesswoman, she'd incorporated it into her networking efforts. She does all the things she needs to do to make acquaintances – social networking, leads groups, networking socials, etc. – but her concentration is on finding her NBFs. Before she can do that, she has to know where to find them.

First, she has to know who to find. Corporate administrative assistants, budget and finance officers, and other similar contacts all feed her business, so all of them are potential NBFs. She wants to go straight to these people rather than waiting for someone to introduce them to her. As Mary begins looking for NBFs, she only wants to consider places where she can meet them directly. She doesn't want to make the mistake she made in elementary school by waiting for them to find her.

After doing a little research, she discovers where some of these people go for lunch or coffee and starts going to those places, herself. She puts herself in the same place and introduces herself to her potential NBFs as the opportunities arise. She also does this with seminars, conferences, and social gatherings her NBFs attend. Sometimes, she doesn't have to introduce herself. Potential NBFs may recognize her from other events or socials and ask her to join in their conversations. Whether they invite her in or she initiates the contact, she is beginning the work of developing a personal relationship that will grow to help in the success of her business.

When interacting with groups and organizations in the local community, she keeps the concept of "blurring" in mind by first finding the thread connecting her to her potential NBFs.

Staying in her office and communicating through social networking sites, email, and other electronic means would be just like sitting under her tree during recess in the fourth grade. Relationships require real interaction in order to grow, so she likes to start these interactions as early in the relationship as possible. Instead of waiting for her NBFs to find her, she goes out to find them.

*****

Early in the development of OfficeScapes' NBF network, I found a Thursday night networking social that proved to be a small gold mine of leads and contacts. I went to these events, paid for whatever my potential NBF was having, and asked questions about their businesses. I listened to what they had to say and left with a pocketful of business cards covered with notes I'd taken. This was effective, but only to a point. If I wanted to catch the big fish, I needed to find a different pond.

In order to break into the networking major leagues, I needed to find NBFs who had more influence and better information. That's why I joined organizations like the El Paso Club and the Pikes Peak Range Riders. Not only do I enjoy these organizations, some of the people I need to connect with enjoy them, too. You have to go where your potential NBFs are, but you should also have a good time while you're there.

Another place I found NBFs for OfficeScapes was inside our competitor's networks. We'd target each of our competitors in an attempt to force them out of business. In a rather Machiavellian fashion, we would initiate and build relationships with people who were providing information to that competitor. Once, I convinced a real estate agent who was providing information to a competitor to work with us. At first, he was reluctant to work with us directly, so he always provided information through his partner. As his partner became more and more successful through the relationship we built with him, the real estate agent witnessed the value of having a close, personal relationship within our NBF network and joined us, abandoning the competitor, which soon closed its doors.

When I took over OfficeScapes, we had a retail side and a contract side. Small business owners and work-at-home individuals who only needed a desk or two and maybe a couple of chairs would come into our retail store and buy these items for themselves. Larger companies that needed furniture for a number of employees would enter into a contract for the delivery and installation of their purchase. The idea, at the time, was the retail side would feed the contract side. In other words, someone who'd bought a desk for their home would refer other customers or come back themselves when their companies grew. This, however, is not what happened. People who purchased a desk or chair for a home office very rarely came back for a larger contract. The retail business and anything associated with it was never going to add to our growth. Keeping this business around would be like Mary waiting for the soccer or basketball girls to introduce her to the girls who played tag. Our potential NBFs were not interested in the retail business, so I cut it and consolidated the business into the contract-only side. Sometimes, going where the potential NBFs are makes you rethink the way you do business.

We had neither revenue nor NBFs in the retail business, but we had both through my connections with the El Paso Club and the Pikes Peak Range Riders. In order to make new friends, you have to know where to look.

SUMMARY

RULE 4: <u>To be friends, you have to have something in common.</u> An NBF relationship is a personal relationship, so you must be able to enjoy your time with them. It is also a business relationship, so your NBFs must be in a position to help your business. This requires blurring the lines between business and pleasure.

RULE 5: <u>To meet new friends, you have to know where to look. NBFs are not going to find you.</u> You must go out and find them. In order to do this, you must know who they are or where they like to hang out. Social media and networking socials will only get you so far. You must take the extra step to find the NBFs who will take your networking efforts to the next level.

CHAPTER THREE

"Life's too short to spend time with jerks."

*Lots of people want to ride with you
in the limo, but what you want is
someone who will take the bus with
you when the limo breaks down.*
—Oprah Winfrey

General Douglas MacArthur once remarked, "Upon the fields of friendly strife are sown the seeds that, upon other fields, on other days will bear the fruits of victory." Johnny learned a lot about life from playing hockey and being part of a team. He learned everyone had to contribute in order for the team to be successful, and if a member was more concerned with himself than the team, they would all fail. As an adult,

41

Johnny treats his community as his team and enjoys working with others to make the community shine.

Johnny also learned fair play on the ice. He watched the 1980 U.S. Olympic men's hockey team play Czechoslovakia on the way to a miraculous gold medal victory. In the game against Czechoslovakia, he saw a Czech player take a cheap shot and injure a U.S. player. He then saw coach Herb Brooks shout across the ice, "I'll bury that god damn stick right in your throat!" Johnny feels the same way about unethical business practices as Herb Brooks felt about cheap shots on the ice.

When building an NBF network, you must keep in mind not everyone is going to be interested in helping you. Life's too short to spend time with jerks, so don't waste your time with people who are only out for themselves.

RULE 6

"Short-timers" are only friends when the time and environment suit them.

In middle school, Johnny's dad always bought season tickets for the local college's hockey team. Johnny was one of the best players in his junior league and always loved going to the games. His father also let him bring one friend to each game they went to see.

One year, a new kid in school found out Johnny invited friends to the hockey games and, because he was a big fan, became friends with Johnny. Even though Johnny usually invited teammates from his junior hockey league, he liked the new kid and invited him to a game. They both had fun and got to know each other a little better. Johnny thought he was making a new friend.

After the season ended and the new kid knew there were no more games scheduled, he started drifting away from Johnny. After a few weeks, Johnny was lucky if the new kid even said "hi" between classes. As long as there were no games, the new kid had no reason to be Johnny's friend.

This irritated Johnny at first, but when the next hockey season came around, the kid came back and wanted to be friends again. He apologized for ignoring Johnny for so long and assured him this time he really wanted to be friends. Reluctantly, Johnny invited him to another game, but just like the previous season, the kid stopped hanging out with Johnny once the season ended.

Johnny never invited the kid to another game, despite protests and assurances that this time would be different. Johnny'd had enough and wasn't going to waste any more time. For Johnny, going to the hockey games was a fun way to spend time with his friends, and this kid wasn't interested in friendship. He was only in it for his own enjoyment.

*****

Johnny's success as a small business owner in a medium-sized city is built upon long-term relationships supporting the community as a whole. This helps make the community grow and thrive, which in turn, allows his business to grow and thrive. It also helps protect his business from economic downturns, because he and his NBFs take the time and make the effort to help one another. His NBF network is a community within itself built on trust and support established over time.

When the economy is good and businesses are thriving, many people want "in" on Johnny's network. In the past, he's even tried letting these people in because he thought they might have something valuable to offer. Very often, they did. Short-term value, however, is no fair trade for long-lasting support.

As the economy inevitably fluctuates, the short-timers slowly fade away, just like the kid in middle school who disappeared after hockey season. Unlike the rest of Johnny's network, they're not around to support one another when contracts became scarce. Many times, these short-timers will fail due to lack of support. It's ironic that the very connections they need to survive are the ones they abandon to look for a better environment.

In the end, Johnny's company, and those within his NBF network, can all succeed because of the trust that comes from being committed to the long term and not instant gratification.

*****

Having the reputation of being a connector in the community often makes me the target for short-timers out for a big short-term payoff. Early on, I was willing to give people the benefit of the doubt, as Johnny did with the new kid who wanted to go to the hockey games. Experience, though, has taught me how to identify, and thus avoid, these predators. I once met a short-timer who seemed like a nice enough person, at the time. I wrote out a list of leads for him, hoping to begin building a relationship. Not long after that meeting, one of my NBFs approached me with a list of leads he'd recently obtained. When I looked at the list, I immediately recognized it. The short-timer had photocopied the list I'd given him, leaving the entire thing in my handwriting. All he'd done was replace my letterhead and logo with his own. He then distributed the list in an attempt to gain favor quickly with others in the community. Not only did he lose my trust, he lost the trust of everyone who recognized my handwriting.

People who have a stake in the success of the community are far more fun to work with and easier to trust. It's easy to find something in common when you're not focused on yourself. Short-timers are only concerned with their own interests. They don't make good NBFs and are not worth the time and effort needed to network with them.

RULE 7

"Poachers" are only friends when they have a specific goal they need you to help them achieve.

Rivalries fuel college sports, and college hockey has more than its fair share of rivalries. This fact wasn't lost on the students at Johnny's middle school. While most of the students who liked hockey cheered for the "home team," others followed one of the home team's rivals. Some of Johnny's closest friends even cheered against him when their favorite team came to town.

One member of Johnny's junior hockey league was a big fan of one of these rivals. He didn't know Johnny very well, but he did know Johnny invited other kids to hockey games. When hockey season came around, he got friendly with Johnny in the hopes of being invited to his team's game. He talked to Johnny after the league games, casually asked about the tickets, chatted with Johnny, and generally acted as though he wanted to be Johnny's friend.

Johnny thought this kid was a good potential friend, so he invited him to the game. The kid was ecstatic about the opportunity to see his team play. He thanked Johnny repeatedly and was exceptionally kind in the days leading up to the game.

At the game, however, the kid seemed forget who brought him there. He started "trash-talking" Johnny and putting Johnny down because he liked the home team. When Johnny's team got behind late in the game, Johnny's father had to force the kid to sit down and be quiet because other fans were complaining. Even though Johnny's team won with a last second goal, it wasn't enough to quiet the kid.

Once outside, the kid became nice again and thanked Johnny and his dad for bringing him. He even apologized for getting "a little carried away." He'd spent the whole game insulting Johnny, the person who invited him in the first place, and acting with complete disregard for everyone else watching the game. He was going to enjoy it the way he wanted to, no matter how many people he stepped on along the way. Because of his behavior, Johnny never invited him to another game.

*****

Sometimes, a big deal comes up that could involve Johnny and his NBFs. During these times, businesses from the surrounding area, especially larger cities, want to get in on the action.

Johnny and his NBFs cheer for the home team. They work together to make their community thrive, not to support some larger city or out-of-state interests. These outsiders only want to get to know you or offer you deals when there's a big reward on the other side for them. They cheer for the rival teams and will only be your friend long enough to get into the game.

Once the poachers are in the stadium—once they become part of your network—they're only out for themselves. They take whatever they can get without any respect for the person who got them there. They have no interest in the home team's success and only celebrate their own team's victories and scores. In the end, they don't care what kind of mess they've left behind because it's not their community. They have no long-term stake in it, nor do they have any true friends who do.

When the job is complete – when the poachers have left the stadium – they politely shake Johnny's hand and say things like, "It got a little rocky there for a while," or "It was a pleasure doing business with you," as though they want to maintain a relationship in case something new comes up in which they might be interested.

Johnny's experiences in middle school taught him something different. The businesses that come in with no local ties are usually looking to take advantage of him to achieve their own goals. That's not what a middle-school friendship is about, and it's not what an NBF relationship is about, either.

*****

Colorado Springs is home to Peterson Air Force Base, the U.S. Air Force Academy, the U.S. Army's Fort Carson, Cheyenne Mountain Air Force Station, Schriever Air Force Base, and many of the defense contractors who support such a large military contingent. The military is a large part of the business in this city, and some of the associated contracts can be lucrative.

Poachers from Denver and from out-of-state always have an eye on these contracts, ready to come in and grab as many as they can before driving or flying back to their own communities. They know they need local contacts to get in on these contracts, and because I have a reputation as being a connector, I am always in their crosshairs.

I've seen what these companies can do to their customers and to the communities they infiltrate, so I am wary of letting too many of these outsiders into my network. People I work with need to have a dedication to the community equal to or greater than my own. Doing what's best for the community in the long term is more important to your long-term success than doing what may be good for you in the short term.

When I work on a job, I try to surround myself with my NBFs. If we all work together to make the entire job a positive experience for the customer, we not only make ourselves look good, we make the entire community look good. That leads to a higher level of success for everyone in my network, which leads to more opportunities for OfficeScapes. I'll talk about this in more detail in future chapters, but for now, just remember poachers aren't interested in this connection between success and community and will tear it down if it suits their bottom line.

RULE 8

Fair play breeds loyalty; foul play breeds contempt.

When Herb Brooks shouted across the ice to the Czech player who'd injured one of his players, people saw an attitude toward unsportsmanlike conduct that made them feel good. Johnny's dad cheered at this almost as loud as when the team scored a goal. He taught Johnny fair play, both on the ice and off, and never to tolerate unsportsmanlike conduct.

Johnny's coach had the same attitude toward unsportsmanlike conduct, but not all the coaches or players in the junior hockey league believed in fair play. Johnny's coach always wanted to beat these teams in order to send the message that cheap shots will never make a winning team. Before games against these teams, the coach would read their rosters, pointing out all of their stats. He'd let them know who the best players and the least-skilled players were, as with any team, but he'd also point out how many penalty minutes they'd had, how many of the various penalties they'd earned, and even how many penalties he'd seen that were never called. This fired up Johnny and his teammates, and they played some of their best hockey against these teams, making them one of the highest-ranked teams in the league.

Johnny learned to keep unscrupulous players off his team and not to accept that kind of conduct from anyone else.

*****

Johnny's dedication to excellence helps keep jerks out of his business. He's learned to avoid them in his networking efforts, but now he has to deal with them in the form of his competition. He hates losing a bid, but he hates it even more when the other company wins the contract by cheating the customer.

First, Johnny had to make his company a top-notch service provider in the market. Simply being the best at what he does, providing the highest quality customer service before and after the sale, will be enough for Johnny to put some of these unethical companies out of business. Others, though, may have some financial backing from a parent company or may be able to put up a good front. Unethical companies that have these things going for them need special attention.

Johnny uses the lessons from time in junior hockey league to take on unethical competitors and put them out of business. He gathers his sales teams and lets them know the details about what's happening inside the target company, just as his coach had gone through the details of the opposing teams' rosters. He turns every contract into a sporting event, firing up his team to put in the extra effort necessary to take the contract out from under the competitor's nose. When they win a contract against one of these companies, they celebrate the victory as a team.

Johnny is dedicated to the community, as is reflected in his choice of NBFs, so he sees putting unethical companies out of business as a service to the community, in addition to reducing the amount of competition in the market. When his colleagues and NBFs feel the same way about the community, it's easy to get their help and support when targeting an unethical company for closing.

*****

The cadets at the U.S. Air Force Academy live under an honor code: "We will not lie, steal, or cheat, nor tolerate among us anyone who does." The other service academies have similar codes. I especially like the last half of that statement because it goes beyond being honorable and forces you to eliminate lying, cheating, and stealing from your community.

When I was building OfficeScapes, I watched as several competitors cheated their customers in contract bids. They would leave vital elements out of a contract in order to enter the lowest bid, but would have to add these things back in after the customer awarded the contract in order to complete it. Sometimes, they even priced the add-in higher than if it had been part of the original bid. Not only did they steal business from their more honest competitors by lying to their customers, they cheated the customer out of money by adding in items at a higher margin, after the fact. I could not tolerate this behavior in my community, so I decided to do something.

Like Johnny and his hockey coach, I wanted to target my unethical competitors and get my team fired up about taking them down. One of the things I did was rent a tour bus, the kind with a microphone in the front and speakers throughout, big enough for my employees. We all got on the bus and drove to the target company's main office building. We parked in their parking lot, and I stood in the front of the bus with the microphone and told them everything I knew about the company and its sales force. I highlighted their unethical practices and explained in detail why that particular business should cease to exist. Like I described in the introduction of this book, I saw these efforts as a form of warfare and I wanted my troops to have all the latest intelligence on the enemy before I sent them off into battle.

I also told them about the good in the company during these expeditions. Designers, installers, and other employees who excelled in their positions were resources we needed to access and obtain. I painted a picture of what our company would be like and how our business would grow once this one closed its doors and we hired the best of their employees. Putting these competitors out of business helped our business grow, gave us the best employees, and raised the amount of respect our customers had for the industry as a whole.

RULE 9

*Long-term friends are more
fun than short-term jerks.*

Going to hockey games was both a pleasure and a learning experience for Johnny. He enjoyed the excitement of the games and he also learned moves, techniques, and plays by watching the experienced players, which helped improve his own game. When Johnny invited his friends and teammates, their shared interests made the game mutually entertaining.

He and his friends enjoyed the popcorn and sodas his dad always bought, and they often tried to see who could shout the loudest when the team scored a goal. Dad usually won. They all dug their fingernails into the seats during last-minute power plays that could either win or lose the game. To Johnny and his friends, hockey was the most exciting thing on earth.

Just as his dad and his coach taught him, Johnny paid close attention to the individual players during these games. With the help of Johnny's dad, he and his friends would dissect the plays to figure out why they'd worked or why they'd failed. After the games, Johnny liked to get his street hockey gear and go to the park to practice what he'd seen during the game. Many times, his friends who'd gone with him would go to the park with Johnny.

When Johnny went to the games with kids who weren't interested in being his friend, they weren't as fun. Sometimes was so busy explaining the rules he'd miss a good play. Other times, the kid didn't like the yelling contests or couldn't understand when Johnny passionately talked about the more technical aspects of the game. With short-timers, poachers, and other people not interested in Johnny, as well as the game, the games were no fun at all.

Johnny learned if you spend time with people who aren't interested in being your friend, you will not have fun, but if you spend time with friends who are interested in you and have something in common, you will have fun.

*****

Johnny remembers the importance of having something in common with his friends when he starts building new relationships in his business network. He joins a few local groups to meet new contacts, and his experiences vary greatly.

One group meets every other week for lunch, and although it's an open group, the long-time members are cold toward newcomers. Johnny is unsure about the group and only attends because it has a reputation for providing good information. Many of the group members don't like what they refer to as "violent barbaric sports," so when they learn about Johnny's passion for hockey, he decides it would be best not to return to the group.

Another "happy hour" group meets once a month. Many people in Johnny's industry attend the group, so he's able to "talk shop" and get some good bits of information. He likes going, but never really gets to know anyone on a personal level. Many times, short-timers and poachers infiltrate these meetings, so he always has to be on his guard when meeting new people in the group.

Johnny thinks about what he enjoys, which is hockey, and how to turn that into a networking opportunity. Ultimately, he joins the local college hockey team's boosters' club. He meets people there who can help him in his business and, at the same time, give him free tickets to some of the games. He spends more time at boosters' activities and makes more connections there than any other networking outlet.

The lunch group's members are only looking out for their reputations, while the "happy hour" group's members are usually only out for their own bottom lines. The hockey boosters are all part of their group for hockey, and everyone has a genuine interest in one another through this common connection. Being a part of the boosters is lucrative as far as business is concerned, but it's also fun.

*****

Life's too short to spend time with jerks, especially in your NBF network. Remember, an NBF is someone with whom you have a long-term relationship. That relationship should be based on helping each other first, as you will see in the next chapter. People who are only out for themselves make business difficult and make trust impossible. It's just not worth the headaches.

Later, you will read about how walking out of a meeting with one good lead you didn't have before is a success. One of my NBFs who knew about this rule stopped me in the hallway after just such a meeting and asked if I'd gotten the one piece of information I didn't already know about. I smiled and told him I hadn't, but I excited to discover that finding leads had become a game for people in my network. It was like a contest to see who could get a lead I hadn't heard about into my hands before the others. People were having fun trying to find the best leads in the market and getting them to me as quickly as possible. With friends like that, success is inevitable.

SUMMARY

RULE 6: <u>"Short-timers" are only there when the time and environment suit them.</u> Short-timers can also be called "fair-weather friends." You want friends who are interested in you for the long-term, not in their own short-term gains.

RULE 7: <u>Poachers are only friends when they have a specific goal they need you to help them achieve.</u> Poachers are users. They will step on you and anything else to achieve their goals and satisfy their bottom lines. You want friends who are interested in helping you help your community. Trust comes more readily to a relationship based on higher goals.

RULE 8: <u>Fair play breeds loyalty; foul play breeds contempt.</u> "We will not lie, steal, or cheat, nor tolerate among us anyone who does." You can never be a good friend if you lack integrity and you can never have a friend in someone else who lacks integrity.

RULE 9: <u>Long-term friends are more fun than short-term jerks.</u> The point of a business relationship is long-term enjoyment that also helps your business succeed. Success gained from jerks is hard-won and short-lived. Success from your NBFs should be a natural course of the relationship.

CHAPTER FOUR

Have Something to Give

*The man who will use his skill and
constructive imagination to see how
much he can give for a dollar, instead
of how little he can give for a dollar, is
bound to succeed.*

—Henry Ford

While Johnny was learning how to deal with jerks,
Mary was learning about not becoming one. The jerks Johnny
dealt with all wanted to take more than they were willing to
give. Although Mary didn't take advantage of her friends, she

limited the growth of her relationships by not understanding some simple rules about giving.

Mary liked her best friends and wanted to invite them all to a sleepover at her house one weekend. Mary was excited about the event and eagerly awaited her friends' arrival at school on Monday morning so she could ask if they wanted to come. When the first friend arrived, Mary ran and immediately invited her to the party. The friend seemed excited, at first, but then asked, "What are we going to do?"

Besides being shocked and a little devastated, Mary was confused. She thought just having a sleepover would be enough to make her friends want to come. All she wanted was to get her friends together at her house, but her friends seemed to want more. If she was going to have a successful sleepover, she had to have something to give.

RULE 10

You get more from listening than from talking.

Mary's mother had always said, "God gave you two ears and one mouth so you can listen twice as much as you talk." Usually Mary would roll her eyes and walk away, but now she was beginning to see the value of that advice. Her friends were always talking about the things they liked, and Mary was always ready to jump into the conversation. As she began to listen, though, she started learning what her friends truly liked.

One of her friends had just started voice lessons and loved to sing. Another friend was getting a video game console for her birthday in a couple of months, but she was itching to play the latest game, right now. None of her friends liked potato chips very much, but they all enjoyed some variation of nachos.

Before she could begin giving things, she had to give her time and herself. Listening to what others had to offer meant intentionally taking the focus off herself and letting others be the center of attention for awhile. Armed with the information she gained from sitting back and listening while her friends remained in the spotlight, she prepared invitations for her friends focusing on their individual desires.

＊＊＊＊＊

Mary is just starting to build her NBF network and rarely has any information that would be beneficial to her NBFs, especially those who are "up the food chain," meaning they naturally know about deals before she does just by the nature of their business. Still, she tries to find the people in the best position to help her business and engage them in conversation. She may not have information, but she can at least buy lunch or a drink.

When meeting these higher-level contacts, she starts with a little small talk or social conversation, but she then lets the other person talk while she listens. She writes things down during or after the conversation so she doesn't forget the details and has accurate information to pass on to other NBFs, if necessary.

If the conversation dwindles, she talks just enough to keep it alive. Because she has been listening to what the other person has been saying and allowing the person to be the focus, she can easily direct the conversation and keep it going. She's learned most people don't like silence in the middle of a conversation. If she remains silent after giving input to the conversation, the other person inevitably fills the silence and she begins taking notes again.

When listening to her contacts, she isn't just looking for business information. This person is a potential NBF, not simply a business information source. Mary wants to know about the person's hobbies, family, or anything in which she can take a genuine interest. She is looking for something the two of them have in common upon which she can build a long-term relationship. An NBF relationship is always a friendship first and a business partnership second.

*****

When I was at Xerox, one sales manager took me on a sales call and watched as I babbled on and on with the customer. The next time he took me out, he told me to ask a question and then count to ten in my head before I said anything else. I tried it, but could only get to three or four before I was bursting to say something to fill the silence. The person I was having the conversation with was feeling the same pressure and would always say something before I reached ten. From that, I learned to be comfortable with "pregnant pauses" in conversations because it gives me more opportunity to listen and learn, plus it takes the focus off what I have to say and puts the other person in the spotlight.

One of my first networking outlets after I took charge of OfficeScapes was the Thursday night "happy hour" I mentioned in the chapter on finding friends. I went to the group, found people who would be good NBFs, and struck up a conversation. I bought them a round of whatever they were having and listened to all they had to say, asking a lot of questions to keep the conversation going. I usually came away from those Thursday night meetings with five or six business cards covered in notes I'd taken. I'd never have collected that much information if I'd done all the talking.

During these conversations, I'd also collect personal information like what the person did for fun, what his or her family was like, or anything that might reveal a little bit of common ground. Just getting a person's birth date and sending a card can create a positive impression and go a long way toward building a relationship. Remember, first and foremost, you are trying to make best friends.

Some may try to argue this is some kind of manipulation. This would be true for short-timers, poachers, and the like, but not for NBFs. The interest you take in an NBF must be genuine in order for the relationship to grow. Doing these things as a checklist to higher profits will bring you neither friends nor profits. Doing these things because you have a genuine interest in the other person will bring to you both friends and profit.

RULE 11

*Whatever you give must have value
to the person receiving it.*

Armed with the knowledge gained from listening to
her friends, Mary went out once again with her invitations. For
the girl who liked to sing, Mary bought a musical invitation
and included a list of songs she had available on her karaoke
machine. For the girl who wanted to play the video game,
Mary included a picture of herself playing the game, but with
no one at the second controller. She did similar things for each
of her friends, and for all of them, she included the list of
ingredients her mom was getting for a "make your own
nachos" table.

Each girl was excited about all the things she would do
at the sleepover, and each girl was impressed Mary had
personalized all the invitations to make the event something
they could each enjoy in their own way. The first time Mary
tried to have the sleepover, she was only concerned with her
own enjoyment. When she had something meaningful and
valuable to offer each girl, all the girls, including Mary, had a
good time.

*****

Being so low on the food chain is frustrating at times for Mary. If she had the kind of information those above her were able to access, she'd easily be able to give all her friends exactly what they need. She knows her NBFs well enough to give them the right information when it's available, but getting that information can be difficult, because she has very little to offer in return. To get it, she has to get creative about what she has to give.

The simplest thing to give is a meal or a drink. Some people like the chance to get away from work and just chat from time to time. Mary recalls one friend who wanted to come to her sleepover just to get away from her annoying little brother for a few hours. A chance to get away is one thing Mary can give that would have value to anyone, without regard for their place in the food chain.

Some people, especially those trying to break into the higher societal tiers, enjoy exposure. They want to be "seen." Mary joined the local country club, where all the local business and political leaders like to have lunch. The club has a "members-only" policy for its dining room, so when she invites non-members, it's a real opportunity for her guests to be "seen." Many people who would roll their eyes at the local lunchtime hot spot or a cup of coffee at a nearby coffeehouse jump at the chance to have lunch with her at the country club.

When Mary has a meeting with one of her NBFs, she always has two or three leads ready to give. She goes through all the leads and other information she's collected and selects the ones most useful to the person she's meeting. She knows which part of town her NBF prefers to work, the type of work her NBF prefers to get, and even the others within her network with whom this NBF prefers to work. Because she knows all this information about her NBF, she never gives a useless lead to anyone with whom she's connected. Mary shares what she has with those who will appreciate it most. As a result, her NBFs have more respect for her, and even though she isn't expecting anything in return, they are more likely to give her valuable information because she is going out of her way to be helpful.

*****

"Giving" is the secret to any NBF relationship, but it can't be giving for the sake of giving. What you give must be valuable to the person receiving it. This is why minor league networking will never lead to the kind of success possible with an NBF network. Networking socials and social networking rely on volume. If you swap enough leads, or interact with enough people, you'll eventually find gold. Like I mentioned in the introduction, I am a member of a local leads group, and in the 14 years since I took over OfficeScapes, that group has produced two leads that actually brought money into the business.

Each time I meet with an NBF or a potential NBF, I have several leads ready to share. In order to set yourself up as a credible connector, you must show you have access to a number of different leads and to leads that have a high value. I usually have a few easy leads to demonstrate quantity, but I also include one or two premium leads to demonstrate quality. The easy leads may or may not have significant value to my NBF, but the quality leads show I am willing to give away things that have true value.

This was difficult when I was just starting out. Sometimes, I'd invite a potential NBF out for lunch, as Mary did, but other times, I wanted to up the value. For those occasions, I sent a personal gift along with an invitation to dinner. Many people gave me good leads during that time just because I was trying to be a nice guy. I wasn't hounding them for information, nor was I barraging them with business talk. I tried to become their friend and demonstrate that friendship by sharing things that were valuable to them.

People in business enjoy little things, like a call on their birthday just to say, "Happy Birthday." I like to dress it up a little to make it more personal and more meaningful.

Sometimes, I call NBFs and yodel "Happy Birthday" into their voicemail. One NBF liked it so much he asked me to yodel "Happy Birthday" for their boss during a staff conference call with the boss's office in New York. I am also a trained auctioneer and have recited a room full of people's birth dates, auction-style. It's something I enjoy, but more importantly, it's something my NBFs enjoy and remember.

Ultimately, you want to trade those "perfect" leads, but in the meantime, you have other things of value you can give. Friendship, entertainment, and meals are all ways to give something with value to your NBFs.

RULE 12

Always expect to give more than you receive.

Like most of the other kids in school, Mary and her friends exchanged cards with one another on holidays. Sometimes, one of her friends would forget to bring cards or didn't have enough allowance money saved, but Mary didn't mind. She knew her friends still liked her and would exchange cards when the next holiday came around.

One girl in Mary's class gave her a card for a holiday and seemed happy when she took it. Mary didn't know the girl very well, but they got together later and talked. They discovered each had the same video game console and over the next few weeks started trading games the other didn't have. Sometimes, they'd agree to trade a game or two, but usually, one girl would bring a game to the other to try just because she thought the other would like it. The giver wouldn't expect to get a game in return; she just wanted her friend to enjoy the one she gave.

Another girl in the class once gave Mary a card for a holiday. She never tried to get to know Mary, who knew that some kids just gave cards to be noticed. This girl turned out to be even worse than those kids. When Mary was planning her sleepover, the girl came to her and asked what they'd be doing, what time it started, and other things that annoyed Mary. Mary finally asked why she was asking all these questions, and the girl told her she should get an invitation because of the card she gave Mary on the previous holiday. Because she gave Mary the card, she believed she deserved an invitation to the sleepover so they'd be "even." Mary didn't like feeling forced to invite someone, so she avoided the annoying girl and had a very enjoyable sleepover without her.

*****

Mary runs into many people who believe life is a zero-sum game, meaning every time someone does something nice for you, you are somehow obligated to do something nice in return. They will give Mary leads and expect the same quality leads from her. When Mary doesn't, or isn't able, to provide that kind of lead, they become irritated and refuse to share any more information until she "pays up." Mary calls these people the "give and take" crowd. They'll give her all the information she needs as long as they can take all they need in return.

Mary prefers to work with the "give and receive" crowd. These people are more like Mary's friends in school who traded cards or video games with her. They don't believe life is a zero-sum game that requires payback for every good deed. Instead, they believe people should "pay it forward." They view each good deed done in the present as an investment that will pay greater dividends in the future. Mary gives information freely to her NBFs knowing someday they will do the same for her, but not expecting it of them. She gives her NBFs the best information she has and receives whatever they freely give her.

One of the things Mary likes about paying forward is she can trust the information she's receiving from others. She knows her NBFs are not weighing the leads they're giving her against what they believe they'll get in return. People who do so think their return on investment is measured in terms of the information received vs. the information shared. Mary and her NBFs believe their return on investment is measured in the strength and longevity of the relationships they are building. What that relationship can bring through its duration is far greater in value than any of the individual leads she has to share.

When Mary was starting out, she gave a lot of time, gifts, and leads in order to establish relationships. She didn't receive much out of these maturing relationships, but despite this, she continued to give. Since developing her NBF network, she often has more information than the people with whom she meets. That means she is still giving more than she is receiving.

In a zero-sum game, if you give more than you receive, you're in the red. Fortunately, paying forward has brought about a much better return for Mary. Not only has her business succeeded over the years, she has many good friendships that will be a part of her life, even when the business is done.

*****

This idea of paying it forward, or give and receive, is probably the most vital part of developing NBF relationships.

It shows you are interested in the other person's best interests and are willing to trust they will look out for yours. Partnerships are built upon give and take, but friendships are built upon give and receive.

Giving more than you receive means you give more quality as well as quantity. When I go into a meeting with my NBFs, I always try to have at least three leads tailored to their specific needs. I put myself in their shoes and think about how I can best serve them with the information I have. For instance, I might have an NBF who is a real estate broker and prefers to work only in the north side of town, so I'll pick out the best leads I have on the north end of town. I may also have an NBF who is a general contractor specializing in "tenant-finish" jobs, where the basic building structure is already in place and the customer is restructuring or refinishing the interior areas of the building. I'm not going to give this NBF a pile of leads that all require new construction.

Many times, you should expect to give more than you receive just because of the circumstances. Like Mary, most people find themselves working harder to make new friends early in their networking efforts. You have to give more than you receive in order to establish trust, build your reputation as a connector, and start building the relationship. As time goes on and you develop your reputation as a connector, you will discover, at some point, you have more information than most of the people you meet. In that case, pay it forward. Think about how to serve them now, and when they have something you need, they'll serve you back.

What you give and how much you give should not be based on what you can get in return. It's based on trust and respect developed over time. You're not going to pass off all your leads to an NBF you're just getting to know. Likewise, you're not going to hold back your best leads from an NBF who's served you well for many years. I'll cover this in more detail in a later chapter about ranking your NBFs. In both cases, and every one in between, always expect to give more than you receive.

SUMMARY

RULE 10: <u>You get more from listening than from talking.</u>
The first thing you can give your NBFs is a friendly ear. Take the focus off yourself, let them talk, and take in all they have to say.

RULE 11: <u>Whatever you give must have value to the person receiving it.</u> Giving for the sake of giving is minor league networking. It takes time, effort, and good listening skills to determine what your NBFs find valuable and then provide it. Things with intrinsic value are just as useful as the information you share.

RULE 12: <u>Always expect to give more than you receive.</u>
Life is not a zero-sum game. Pay it forward and you will reap dividends in business and the relationship. Put yourself in your NBF's shoes, determine how best to serve them, and they will serve you back.

CHAPTER FIVE

Building Relationships

You can make more friends in two months by becoming interested in other people than you can in two years by trying to get other people interested in you.
—Dale Carnegie

If making friends takes a lot of work, keeping them takes that much more. Not only must you continue listening, giving, and reaching out to new people, you must continually renew the relationships you have in order to keep them fresh. We've all lost track of people over the years because we failed to make the effort to maintain the relationship. Some of these relationships may have been close—best friends we thought we'd be with forever. This is why websites such as

Classmates.com and Reunion.com are able to exist; many people have relationships that have faded over time.

When your friends are NBFs who feed your business, failure to keep the relationships going can starve your business. Without these relationships, your business cannot excel and, in many cases, cannot succeed. No matter how well you manage your business or how efficient your processes, people are the key to your business's success. Business is not about the day-to-day tactical things you do, although these are still important and necessary. Business is about relationships.

RULE 13

People who don't enjoy your company don't make good friends.

Mary enjoyed inviting her friends to her house when she was in middle school. Some were friends she'd known for a couple of years, while others were recent additions to her circle of friends. Some of these new friends would eventually become part of her "inner circle," while others would remain casual friends, and still others would fade away.

When Mary invited friends over, she liked to catch up with the latest gossip going around the school. She and her friends would usually gather in the kitchen and raid the refrigerator while talking about parents, teachers, other girls, and of course, boys. After this time together, Mary and her friends would start doing whatever else they'd planned for the day or the weekend. If a girl wanted to become one of Mary's best friends, she had to be able to enjoy Mary's company, first, and the things they did together, second.

Sometimes, girls would come over and want to get started with the plans for the day without enjoying a snack together and exchanging gossip. While the other girls were discussing everything from parents to classmates, this girl continuously interrupted the conversation trying to urge the girls into action and away from the gossip. Mary would not be likely to invite her back because she seemed more focused on her own interests than sharing time with Mary and her friends.

In order to be Mary's friend, a girl had to be interested in Mary as a person. Otherwise, Mary assumed the girl was only using her to get to something else. The girls interested in Mary reaped the benefits of the friendship while she shut out those who ignored her.

*****

Mary likes spending time with her NBFs. Most of the day, she and her NBFs are busy running their businesses, so Mary prefers meeting for breakfast or lunch. That way, she can take the time to reestablish the relationship before getting down to business. When she was in middle school, she liked to spend time catching up on the school gossip. Now, she likes to catch up on what's been going on in the lives of her NBFs. By showing this level of interest in the person, she is able to develop the relationship and then reap the benefits that come along with it. Without this genuine interest, she knows she will end up with neither friend nor benefit.

First, Mary likes to send a personal reminder by voicemail the day before the meeting, or email or text the day of the scheduled meeting. In the message, she says she was simply calling (or writing) to confirm the meeting and to say she is looking forward to it. By confirming the meeting, she gently reminds her NBF about the meeting and reassures her NBF she will be there. Because she made the confirmation herself, and not through a personal or administrative assistant, her NBF is more likely to focus on the relationship as well as the substance of the meeting. Because she says she's looking forward to the meeting, she reassures her NBF she is interested in sharing time as well as information and leads.

If Mary makes the effort to reestablish the relationship with a confirmation message, she could destroy that progress by showing up late for the meeting. Arriving late tells her NBFs she is not concerned about their time and whatever she is doing is more important than meeting them. To prevent this, Mary leaves early and plans for traffic so she arrives a few minutes before her NBFs and is waiting to greet them and shake their hands.

When Mary meets with her NBFs, she uses rules similar to those she used in middle school. To begin with, she always tries to go to places where you must sit down and order from a menu. Buffet lines and waiting at the counter do not allow the kind of conversation she needs to reestablish the relationship. She also tries to find places that are quieter than most so she and her NBF do not have to shout to be heard.

Once they sit down, Mary asks about her NBFs' hobbies, family, or anything that will help reestablish a personal link with her NBF. She listens intently and answers questions her NBF asks about her personal life. She keeps this up until the food arrives. At that point, she feels they've had enough time to reconnect, so she allows business conversation to begin. Once the meal is over, she is ready to tie up any loose ends from the conversation. By taking the time to reconnect, she reestablishes a personal connection, so when it's time to talk business, her NBFs are willing to be more open with her. By being a friend first, she is able to enjoy all the friendship has to offer.

*****

It's said, about golf, you don't begin talking about business until the back nine. The front nine is for reestablishing your relationships. Personally, I'm not much of a golfer, but I do enjoy a good meal, so I have adapted this rule of golf to my breakfast or lunch meetings with NBFs. I usually schedule a meeting at a restaurant where you order from a waiter or waitress at your table. Like Mary, I believe this is much more conducive to conversation than buffet-style restaurants or waiting in line at a counter. It's not about the food; it's about the friendship. From the time we sit down until the time the meal comes, I try to catch up on the relationship with my NBF. It's easier than jumping straight into business and creates the right atmosphere before we move on into the heavier topics. During the meal, we talk business, and after the meal, we address anything that needs following up. By working to refresh the relationship, the business discussions become more intimate and more productive for both my NBF and me.

Even before the meal, however, I work to make sure I am in the front of my NBF's mind and to reassure him of my interest. If we're meeting for breakfast, I leave a message similar to Mary's the day before on my NBF's voicemail or email. If it's a lunch meeting, I may leave a message the day before or I may send a text the morning of the meeting. The point of the message is to let my NBFs know I am thinking about them.

I also like to arrive a few minutes early for the meeting so I am there to greet my NBF, especially if it's our first meeting. My time is important, but when it comes to making a new best friend, theirs is that much more so. I want to let them know early in the relationship I value their time and can be trusted to be where I say I will be when I say I'll be there. I want them to know up front they are valuable to me as a friend and not just as a stepping-stone to some selfish interest.

RULE 14

*People who don't respect your
time don't make good friends.*

Mary's mom limited the number of friends she could have over at any one time, so Mary often had difficulty deciding which of her best friends and which of her new friends to invite. She always invited at least one of her "inner circle" friends, but she also wanted to get to know the girls she'd met more recently.

When someone forgot to come or decided to do something else, instead, Mary would not invite that girl back until her other friends had a chance to come over. She didn't think it was fair to invite someone who wouldn't show up when she could have been having fun with a friend who wanted to be there.

Mary also got frustrated when girls showed up late. She couldn't stand missing a juicy piece of school gossip to go answer the door. Once the snacks and talk started, she wanted to stay with it until the group decided to move on. Inevitably, if a girl showed up late, she wanted the girls to fill her in on everything she'd missed. When they did, Mary had to listen to everything over again. Then she felt they were wasting time when they could have been doing something more interesting.

Mary's closest friends respected her time and let her know ahead of time if they couldn't come rather than cancelling at the last minute or not showing up. When they did come, they were excited to spend time with Mary and didn't want to be late.

*****

When meeting an NBF, Mary makes an effort to be a little early to show she respects her NBF's time. In return, she expects them to respect her time. If someone is repeatedly late, Mary concludes that person is not interested in spending time with her and begins inviting new people to breakfast or lunch in that person's place. In school, Mary's closest friends were always on time because they were excited to be with her. She wants to have the same kind of relationship with her NBFs. Those who are not looking for the same thing are not very likely to become one.

Mary's time is valuable. When someone cancels at the last minute, or simply doesn't show up, they're wasting everyone's time. They waste Mary's time because now she has an available appointment and no time to fill it. She could be meeting another NBF, renewing a friendship and trading valuable leads, but all that is lost due to the no-show. A last-minute cancellation or no-show also wastes the time of her other NBFs who could have benefitted from the meeting.

Like in middle school, Mary doesn't think it's fair to her other NBFs to keep rescheduling someone who doesn't show up, so she makes sure other NBFs get an opportunity to schedule a meeting, first. This sends a message to the person who cancelled. People must respect her time if they want to become her friends. Mary believes, when she has a meeting scheduled with someone, that person should be the most important thing to her for that span of time. She expects no less from her NBFs.

*****

Respecting each other's time is an important part of building an NBF relationship. In the early stages of the relationship, respecting your NBFs' time lets them know you want a stronger relationship and you expect the same from them. As the relationship matures, you shouldn't have to think about respecting each other's time. The nature of the relationship will make you want to meet with the person and will make you excited to see them any time you have the opportunity.

I never reschedule someone who cancels any sooner than two to three weeks out. First, my calendar fills up quickly, so most of the time I couldn't schedule anyone any sooner, regardless. Second, I want to send a message to the person that I'm not playing games and I'm only interested in meeting people who are serious about building a relationship. Wasting my time and that of my other NBFs is not a way to start a friendship. I have to trust you will do what you say you'll do, and not showing up for a scheduled meeting tells me just the opposite. Trust and respect are foundational to a successful NBF relationship.

RULE 15

Best friends always know what to expect.

Mary and her friends liked to get together at one of their houses every couple of weeks on a Friday afternoon. The girls seemed to fall into a routine on these Friday get-togethers. When they visited Mary's house, for example, they would meet after school and walk the few blocks to Mary's house, together. Once there, they went straight to the kitchen to fix after-school snacks and begin the gossip session. Mary's mom wouldn't allow food outside the kitchen or dining room, so the girls finished their snacks before moving on to the den. When everyone was ready, they selected a movie to watch. They often talked throughout the movie, either praising or criticizing it. Once the movie was over, the girls would depart for their respective homes, unless they'd coordinated a sleepover ahead of time. If they had, then a completely new routine began.

When girls who were new to the group came over, they were not aware of the routine and sometimes had to be embarrassingly corrected or guided through the steps. For example, they may have turned down the hallway to the den when everyone else was going to the kitchen, or they may have tried to bring food into the den. When the girls got to the den, the new girls may have wanted to do something other than watch a movie or may have wanted to watch it quietly rather than listen to everyone else's commentary.

As Mary's relationships grew, the girls became accustomed to the routine and Mary did what she could to maintain it. When something happened to disrupt the routine, like the time Mary's mom cleaned the carpet in the den and wouldn't let the girls use it, everything seemed a little "off" as each girl tried to decide what to do, instead.

*****

Whether Mary meets her NBFs once a month or once a quarter, she allows a routine to develop. She already has a routine she tries to enforce during a meal, taking time before the food arrives to catch up on the relationship, but a larger routine sets in, also. Sometimes, it's as simple as meeting the same day, such as the second Tuesday of every month. Other times, it could be as complex as meeting the same day of the month, at the same time, at the same restaurant, and even ordering the same food. As she develops a good relationship with an NBF, the routine develops on its own. It's just like in middle school when her friends came over to her house. They fell into their routine naturally, based on all the things they had in common and their interest in spending time with each other.

If Mary is meeting someone new or if her routine with an NBF is disturbed, the information and conversation never seem to flow as naturally as when she's in the routine. Consistency provides comfort to her NBFs and provides immediate common ground when they meet.

*****

Consistency creates comfort, and comfort leads to openness. The purpose of a friendship is mutual enjoyment, but the purpose of an NBF relationship is mutual enjoyment with information exchange. Given that, openness is something you want to encourage.

I have found meeting an NBF once a month is sufficient to maintain a good relationship. Any more frequently begins to limit the number of NBFs I can meet and is not likely to produce any new information, except, possibly, in a period of rapid economic growth. I'll meet with some

NBFs once a quarter, or even once a year, if it fits the relationship and the level of information they are providing.

I have a breakfast meeting every third Thursday at the same restaurant. For breakfast, I like to meet at 7:30 AM. Seven o'clock is too early for me to be anywhere and 8:00 AM is generally considered the beginning of the business day, so people are more focused on running their businesses than breakfast. With a 7:30 AM breakfast, I can also make a 9:00 AM business meeting or conference call, which I couldn't do with a later start time.

Lunch appointments are similar. I always try to schedule lunch for 11:45 AM. Most people schedule lunch at noon, so by scheduling mine at 11:45 AM, I beat the rush and I have 15 minutes of time with my NBF that is less likely to be interrupted.

My NBFs always get a call or message from me reminding them of our meeting, which is usually scheduled at the same time on the same day at the same location to which they've become accustomed. I am there a few minutes early to greet them. We sit down to order our meals and catch up on personal details. Once the food arrives, we slide smoothly into business conversation and leads information exchange. It becomes a dance, with each person contributing equally to the routine. Building consistency is part of building a relationship. Your best friends should always know what to expect.

RULE 16

Your best friends should always be in the forefront of your mind.

Mary went on vacation somewhere different with her family every summer. For each place she visited, she brought back a souvenir for her best friends. All of her friends had different tastes, so she tried to find something each would enjoy. She wanted her friends to appreciate their gifts and to remember her each time they saw them. She didn't want to give a gift her friends would quickly forget and end up selling in a garage sale the next summer. When her friends received these gifts, they knew Mary cared about them and wasn't trying to buy their friendship.

Mary's friends appreciated how much Mary liked them. They displayed the gifts Mary gave them, so each time they went into their rooms, they had something that reminded them of her. When they went on vacation, or when they were shopping for birthday presents, Mary and her thoughtful gifts were at the forefront of their minds. Mary showed she was always thinking of them and, as a result, they were always thinking of her.

* * * * *

Mary gets a lot of information through her NBF network. Each bit of information she doesn't use for herself is like a gift waiting to be given to another NBF, and just as when she was younger, she always tries to find the right gift for the right person. She knows her NBFs' likes and dislikes, and when she's found the one who can use the information most, she sends it to them. She does this as soon after she receives the information as possible, usually in her car from her phone right after the meeting she's just had. The simple statement, "I was just in a meeting and heard something you might be interested in," before giving her NBF the information works wonders in building the relationship.

When NBFs have been particularly helpful, she likes to reward them to let them know she appreciates their efforts. Some may get a nice dinner, others may get tickets to sporting events or concerts, and still others may get gifts personalized to their particular tastes. Whatever she gives, she wants her NBFs to know they are appreciated, but she also wants to keep herself in the forefront of their minds. Like in middle school, she wants her NBFs to be thinking about her and the relationship than merely about the gift.

*****

In the chapter on having something to give, I concentrated on having something the other person finds valuable, but in an NBF relationship, there's more to it. I could give exotic vacation packages to my best NBFs, but I don't. Although these would have value to many of my NBFs, they're not going to be sitting out all day on the beaches of Maui thinking, "Peter is really a nice guy. I'm glad he thought to give us this trip."

For my NBFs, I try to come up with gifts that have both a value commensurate with the amount of business they've given OfficeScapes and will keep me in their minds as they're enjoying it. My top NBFs sit in Coach leather chairs. I give one of these fine leather chairs to an NBF who's provided OfficeScapes with a large amount of business. If they are consistent, I simply trade out the chair when a newer model becomes available. Every time they sit down at their desk, they think about me.

One general contractor who has provided a substantial amount of business for OfficeScapes over time receives new furniture any time he expands his office or needs some of his old furniture replaced. You can't go into his office without noticing OfficeScapes' presence.

While I don't do exclusive trips, I am fortunate enough to be able to offer our best NBFs things like courtside seats to a Denver Nuggets basketball game. After I take them out to dinner, we go to the game and sit right in the front row. Our NBFs love the opportunity to see the game and be "seen" when the TV cameras pan the team benches.

I also reward less influential NBFs for their contributions to OfficeScapes' success. Colorado College hockey tickets, Colorado Springs Sky Sox baseball tickets, tickets to local attractions, or dinners at fine restaurants in town cost very little compared to the impact they have on a fledgling NBF relationship and are nice ways for me to say "thank you," while keeping myself in the forefront of their minds.

When you have information to give, you shouldn't just dump it on your NBFs. Let them know you were thinking of them and you chose this information specifically to fit their needs. If you gently remind them you are thinking of them, they're more likely to be thinking of you when they have something to give.

Summary

RULE 13: <u>People who don't enjoy your company don't make good friends.</u> People who act as though they'd rather be doing something else or are overly anxious to "cut to the chase" aren't interested in you. They will only be interested in what you have to offer and won't make good NBFs.

RULE 14: <u>People who don't respect your time don't make good friends.</u> People who are repeatedly late, cancel unexpectedly, or simply don't show up for your meetings have things they consider more important than your friendship.

RULE 15: <u>Best friends always know what to expect.</u> Consistency creates comfort, and comfort leads to openness. Let a natural routine form between you and your NBFs as your relationships mature and be consistent with it.

RULE 16: <u>Your best friends should always be in the forefront of your mind.</u> Best friends see opportunities for each other because they are always thinking of each other.

CHAPTER SIX

Building Trust

*I'm not upset you lied to me. I'm upset
that from now on I can't believe you.*
—Friedrich Nietzsche

Learning to trust is one of the most difficult parts of
building a long-term and open friendship. Earning the trust of
another is even more difficult, but that trust is an absolute
necessity. Russian playwright Anton Chekhov wrote, "You
must trust and believe in people or life becomes impossible."
For your business, you must trust people or success becomes
impossible.

Trust is not an all-or-nothing proposition, however.
It's measured, based on the amount and type of experiences

you've shared with the people around you. Cicero taught this lesson when he wrote, "Trust no one unless you've eaten much salt with him." The more positive experiences you share, the more you are able to trust.

Johnny and his friends discovered this as they grew up together and their relationships matured. Along the way, those who couldn't keep their word were cast out, as were those who served themselves at the expense of others. Trust between Johnny's friends was built upon years of giving, receiving, listening, and keeping one another's interests ahead of their own. All of them made mistakes, but they learned from them and made amends when it became necessary. By the time they were well into high school, they knew what to expect from one another and had earned one another's trust.

RULE 17

Never reveal your sources.

As captain of the hockey team, Johnny had access to information no one else on the team had. He became captain, in part, because the coach could trust him. When the coach decided to cut one of the players from the team, Johnny was the first to find out.

After learning about the cut, Johnny thought about another friend who'd wanted to try out for the team, but all the positions had been filled at the beginning of the season. He decided to give his friend a head start on preparing for the tryout. His friend was a good player, but a couple days of extra practice would give him the edge he needed to make the team.

Johnny trusted his friend not to leak the information. Otherwise, he wouldn't have shared it. If either of them had spread the information, the player being cut would have faced embarrassment because the coach wasn't able to tell him until the following afternoon.

When his friend asked where Johnny heard the news, Johnny said, "I'm the team captain.. It comes with the job." This answer satisfied Johnny's friend and ultimately gave him more respect for Johnny. He saw Johnny trusted him with confidential information, but he also saw Johnny was willing to protect his sources, even if there was a risk he would offend his friends. His friend knew Johnny would protect any information he gave with the same dedication. Had Johnny told his friend about the conversation with the coach, he would have actually lost trust with his friend.

*****

As a business leader with many NBF connections, Johnny has access to a lot of inside information. Like a good NBF, he is always thinking of who in his network can use the most recent juicy tidbit he's collected. One day, he finds out about a new deal coming down the pike that would be a perfect fit for a new NBF. When he delivers the information, the NBF is excited about the new opportunity, but is also skeptical. He hasn't known Johnny long enough to have built up a large amount of trust. Johnny accepts this because he understands, to take from Cicero, they haven't yet "eaten much salt" together.

The NBF asks Johnny where he got the information. He wants to verify the information, but Johnny refuses to reveal his source. Johnny reassures his NBF and says, "The information is good. I have an extensive network – a lot of feet on the street. I just know things."

When the deal pans out for the NBF, he remembers the conversation with Johnny and realizes Johnny did the right thing by keeping the source a secret. The NBF got a piece of information while closing this new contract he thought Johnny might find useful. He now has no problem giving the lead to Johnny because he trusts Johnny will protect him as the source.

*****

When you're trading information within your NBF network, most of that information comes with the presumption of confidentiality. You are getting information no one else has from a friend who is simply trying to lend a hand. Like a journalist's source who doesn't want to be named in conjunction with the story, your NBFs usually have some reason they don't want to be identified as the source of the information they give. Betraying that confidence is death to NBF relationships, especially when it gets back to your contact you released his or her name. To build trust in an NBF relationship, you must continuously show you are willing to protect your sources.

Not revealing your sources can be difficult when you're giving information to another NBF who wants to know more. Some NBFs may feel alienated or withdraw from the relationship if you don't tell them where you got the information. To prevent this, you must be ready to reassure your NBFs the information is genuine. I say things like, "I'm just a big juicy grape on the vine. I have many contacts who are always giving me new information" or "I have a lot of contacts–a lot of feet on the street–who give me a lot of good, inside information."

Customers will also want to know the source of your information, especially if you use it for a sales call or similar meeting. Under no circumstances, whatsoever, will I ever reveal a source to a customer. Even if they give me an ultimatum, threatening to leave if I don't tell them, I will still protect my source.

Many times, this customer inquiry falls to my sales staff to answer. In that case, I let them blame me with statements like, "Our boss has a lot of connections and has access to a lot of information throughout the industry. He's a big juicy grape on the vine."

Whether it's a customer or an NBF, you must protect your sources. If a reporter revealed an anonymous source in a news article, the source would never give the reporter any more information. Likewise, in business, if you reveal your sources, your sources will shut down.

RULE 18

*Never give information to people
in competition with each other.*

From the time Johnny told his friend about the slot opening on the hockey team, the friend excitedly prepared for the tryout. Johnny worked with him and suggested they practice at the skate rink downtown rather than at school because other boys who would compete against his friend might have caught on to what was happening. Johnny wanted to give his friend an advantage, so he didn't tell anyone else. If others found out about it, or figured it out for themselves, the advantage would have been lost. Johnny was very careful about who got the information, even incidentally.

The reason Johnny was so protective of the information related to the tryout was an experience he had the year before when he was getting ready to try out for captain of the team. The outgoing captain pulled Johnny aside and told him all the secrets he knew about what the coach expected from a team captain. In the following days, Johnny saw four or five other boys practicing all the same things the captain told him to practice. The outgoing captain had told all of them the same "secrets." Johnny felt betrayed and never had a good relationship with the former captain after that incident. He vowed he would never treat any of his friends the way the captain had treated him.

*****

The lessons from the hockey team stayed with Johnny as he moved up in the business world. He was always receiving information from new sources he would then distribute to his NBFs. He knows who works in which areas of town, who prefers which types of work, and who's hungry for something new. He doesn't want to set two NBFs against each other for one job, so he carefully selects the NBF to whom he will give the information.

If two NBFs work in the same industry or like the same kind of work, he makes a judgment call to determine who should receive the information. Later, when another bit of information comes to him, he'll give it to the other NBF.

Johnny is more interested in long-term relationships than short-term gain for both himself and his NBFs. Giving information to people in the same industry will most likely end up in broken relationships with limited or no long-term gain, just as it did for the captain of Johnny's hockey team.

*****

The people give you information and the people to whom you give it all have networks of their own. If you have two NBFs in the same industry, you can assume they are connected with each other, if only indirectly. This means it is easy for them to figure out if you've given both of them the same information. You can't hide it, so once they discover what you've done, you will lose their trust. Not only will they be reluctant to give you any new information, they will not trust any information from you, either.

In a long-term NBF relationship, you survive on giving and receiving. If you serve your NBFs well by providing solid information and earning their trust, they will do the same for you. When you break that trust and they can no longer accept the information you have to offer, they have no reason to give anything back. Failure to serve your NBFs with integrity ends in the failure of the relationship. With enough failed relationships, your business will inevitably fail.

This rule also applies to the people who give information to me. For example, if a commercial real estate agent gives me a new lead, I will never share that information with another real estate agent. The one who gave the information to me is obviously working the deal himself, so giving the information to another agent would only create competition within my network. Because they are both in the same industry, it wouldn't take much for them to figure out what had happened.

There will eventually be enough information to go around within your network, especially as you build your reputation as a connector. Everyone will eventually benefit from what you have to offer, so you have no need to give the same information to too many people, especially if they're in the same industry.

Rule 19

Keep secrets secret; use the "spill rule."

As the day of the tryout drew nearer, word about the open slot on the team's roster began to spread. The player who'd been cut stopped going to practice and rumors began flying. Johnny continued working with his friend at the downtown rink, but more and more people began to approach Johnny's friend about what they were doing. They knew he was a close friend to Johnny and expected him to know all the details.

Like Johnny, his friend wanted to protect his sources, so he didn't confirm or deny any of the rumors, at first. One day, another boy came to Johnny's friend to ask about the open slot. The boy knew several details the friend had only heard from Johnny, and he knew Johnny hadn't spoken to the boy about the situation. Someone else had to have told him the details about the tryout. Johnny's friend told the boy he'd heard the same thing but didn't say where he'd heard it.

Later that week, several other boys asked Johnny's friend about the tryout. They, too, knew the facts about the situation. It was obvious to Johnny's friend that several people knew the details about the tryout, so he told them the information was valid but was no longer a secret. Anyone thinking he had valuable new information was disappointed to learn it had already "hit the streets."

*****

Johnny incorporates his friend's actions with respect to the hockey tryout into his network relationships. When someone comes to him with information about a new deal, he holds that information close to the chest and doesn't reveal it to anyone unless he is sure it is already communally available. The rule he has for exclusive information is to keep it private and use his network and influence to help his NBF close the deal or win the contract. This type of information is usually only available in the early stages of a project, which gives Johnny's NBFs a big advantage. If the project has a role Johnny's company could fill, then Johnny's NBFs are also helping him get in on the contract.

When Johnny hears about the deal from a second, independent source, he knows a handful of people already know about it. In this case, he feels he can safely tell the new source he, too, has heard the same information. He doesn't reveal any further detail, but he acknowledges and corroborates the information the NBF is bringing to the table.

Finally, when Johnny hears the same information from yet another independent source, he assumes the information is old news and already generally known throughout the industry or his network. Anyone bringing news in this category has nothing of value to give Johnny. To be effective in his business, Johnny needs information in the first two categories. Information in the third category is already available to his competitors, which doesn't give Johnny the kind of advantage he needs.

*****

A general rule of communications I once learned is this: If you tell one person something, you've told one person; if you tell two people, you've told eleven; if you tell three people, you've told the world. This rule is the basis for the "spill rule." If you've heard a piece of information once, you shouldn't share it with anyone because you are the only one who knows. If you hear a piece of information twice, at least ten others have already heard it, so you can corroborate the information. If you hear a piece of information three times, everyone in the industry has access to it, so it's old news and has very little value.

Any time an NBF comes to me with a deal I haven't heard, I considerate it my job to keep the information secret and work with my NBF to close the deal. These deals are part of what makes business fun for me. I feel more like a kid playing a spy game with his friends than a corporate executive. I enjoy working with my NBFs behind the scenes using "secret" information to win the game (close the deal) before the bad guys (the competition) even know the deal exists.

When I've heard a piece of information twice, I am willing to corroborate it. I will not add any new facts to those my NBF has given me. I will simply let the other NBF know the information has validity.

Finally, if I've heard a piece of information three times, I have to assume it has become common knowledge throughout the industry. This most often happens when people give me leads they believe are "new." When they approach me with leads I've heard more than three times, I take them aside and tell them although they think this information is new, I have heard it often enough to believe it has already "hit the streets."

The "spill rule" is a great tool to help you decide how to handle information you get from your NBFs. Handling information properly will help you build trust in your NBF relationships, which will give your NBFs the confidence they need to entrust you with information that is more valuable.

Summary

RULE 17: <u>Never reveal your sources.</u> Many times, your NBFs will give you information on the presumption of confidentiality; "You didn't hear it from me, but…" Never betray that trust by revealing where you got information. Just be a "big, juicy grape on the vine."

RULE 18: <u>Never give information to people in competition with each other.</u> Don't pit your NBFs against one another by giving them all the same information. Don't betray the trust of your NBFs by spreading the information they give you to others in their industry.

RULE 19: <u>Keep secrets secret; use the "spill rule."</u> If you hear a piece of information once, keep it sealed and work with your NBF to win the contract. If you hear it twice, corroborate, but don't elaborate. If you hear it three or more times, it's old news and has little value.

CHAPTER SEVEN

"Bestest" Friends

*Be courteous to all, but intimate with
few, and let those few be well tried
before you give them your confidence.*
                                    —George Washington

You'll never make everyone happy and there's never
enough to go around. These axioms affect all your
relationships, including those with your NBFs. You will
always be making compromises, whether it's deciding who
will get a particular bit of information or who will meet with
you for breakfast next Wednesday morning. A good way to
deal with these compromises is to rank and categorize your
NBFs. In a society constantly trying to be "fair," this may not

seem like the most prudent way to handle your relationships, but in reality, it's something you've done your entire life, whether you've realized it or not.

When you were young, you had friends, but some friends stood out in their relationships with you and earned titles such as "best friend" or "BFF (Best Friend Forever)." If your friends invited you to two different birthday parties on the same weekend and your mom would only let you go to one, you chose your best friend's party over the other one. If you could go to both parties, you brought a personal—and likely more expensive—gift to your best friend.

Dividing your friends into categories is something you probably do in your relationships without even thinking about it. For example, a man may have his "poker buddies" or "golf buddies" in addition to his "work friends," and they may or may not ever meet one another. Ladies may have friends from around the neighborhood or the "Girls' Night Out" group, as well as their work friends, and these are not necessarily the same people.

Ranking your friends helps you decide what kind of information or gifts to give the NBFs who've had the greatest impact on your business, just as it helped you decide what kind of gift to bring to your best friend's birthday party. This kind of measured giving strengthens your relationships with your

NBFs by telling them you recognize and appreciate the magnitude of the things they've done for you. When people feel appreciated, they are more likely to help you in the future.

Johnny learned these lessons early in life and applied them to his relationships in high school. When he went on to become a successful business leader, they became a part of the way he interacted with his NBFs.

RULE 20

Categorizing friends helps you decide who should get which information and which gifts.

As captain of the hockey team in high school, Johnny was popular and had many friends. His closest friends were on the hockey team with him, but Johnny had interests outside hockey he and his teammates didn't always share. He had a number of relationships with people who weren't on the team, ranging from close friendships to mere acquaintances.

Johnny was a fan of the local minor league baseball team. In the summer, when there were no hockey games to attend, he enjoyed going to the baseball games with some of the boys from his neighborhood. Before any of them could drive, they rode their bicycles in a pack to the stadium on Saturday afternoons when the team was playing a home game. When they were older, they piled as many of themselves as possible into the bed of a pickup truck so they only had to pay once for parking and could save their money for hot dogs and souvenirs.

At school, Johnny was involved in a variety of other activities. He and some of his hockey teammates were in the same chemistry class and decided to start a study group during a free period to help ensure no one would be cut from the team due to grades. Most of the people who eventually joined the group neither played hockey nor liked baseball. Some group members hated sports altogether, like Mary, who only came to the group because her best friend did.

Johnny had "hockey friends," "baseball friends," "chemistry friends," and friends in a variety of other categories. Some friends were in multiple categories, like the hockey teammates who were also in the chemistry group. Other friends, even though they shared a mutual relationship with Johnny, would never meet one another.

Johnny didn't force this division among his friends. He shared some things in common with some people and other things in common with others. These different commonalities created the categories, not Johnny. He simply recognized this separation and used it as a tool to build his relationships.

*****

In earlier chapters, you read how Mary narrowed down her search for NBFs by identifying those people who could influence her business based on where they fell within her industry's food chain. Johnny did something very similar in high school. His hockey friends would probably influence him more than any others and have something of greater value to offer him. Johnny's relationships as a businessman also fall out into a set of categories, some of which will naturally have something of higher value to offer.

Johnny has his NBFs divided into his industry's food-chain order, first. Those who will know about a deal before him, just by the nature of their businesses, are in the upper level of the food chain, and those who will find out about a new deal later are in the lower echelons. The NBFs in the upper level will have more influence on his business because knowing about a deal ahead of his competitors is a priority for Johnny. Anyone who can help him in that endeavor is going to be more important to him and his business.

Johnny further separates his friends within the food chain into categories based on the industries they represent.

NBFs from several industries will interface with Johnny on any particular job. While they all work toward the goal of satisfying their customer, they also have their own specific needs when it comes to information Johnny has to offer. Dividing them into groups based on their industries helps him when it comes time to give out information he's collected.

Johnny's NBFs have niche markets in which they prefer to work. Even though two NBFs work in the same industry, they may prefer to work in different parts of town or prefer different specialties within their industries. Johnny keeps these categories in mind, as well, when he is seeking or distributing information.

Other categories exist within Johnny's network. All of them are a result of the commonalities he shares with each of his NBFs. Johnny advances his relationships with his NBFs by recognizing these categories and using them to their mutual advantage.

*****

In my industry, the people with whom I most want to connect are in what I call the "A.C.E." industries–Architectural, Construction, and Engineering. These industries are higher in the food chain than I am and are more likely to know about a deal before me. These NBFs will very often be working with my customers before the customers have seriously considered the details of their office furniture needs. Friends like this can give my business a very big advantage over my competition.

While my "A.C.E." NBFs are very important to the success of my business, I can't ignore the contributions of others who may not be as high on the food chain. Painters, drywallers, flooring installers, and business-to-business vendors have important information or information that will fill in the gaps in the leads I've already collected. I don't expect these lower-level contacts to bring me "silver platter deals," but I still need the information they have and the contacts they can bring.

Within each of these industries, my NBFs have niche markets in which they each like to concentrate. As I've suggested in previous chapters, some of my construction NBFs prefer new construction, some prefer tenant-finish work, some prefer to work government contracts, and others try to avoid government contracts altogether. Some of my real estate NBFs prefer to work in the north part of town, while others prefer a different geographic area. Some prefer industrial buildings, some prefer medical facilities, and others prefer a different sub-specialty.

Knowing the categories my NBFs separate themselves into helps me give the right information to the right person at the right time. Doing so helps me serve my friends better and build stronger relationships. With stronger relationships, my NBFs will be more inclined to help me.

RULE 21

Ranking friends helps you decide who should receive information and gifts that are more valuable.

Johnny's father was always receiving free tickets to various sporting events around town through his business friends. Many times, he gave the tickets to Johnny and his friends to enjoy. When he got baseball tickets, Johnny invited a baseball friend to go with him, but when he got hockey tickets, he invited hockey friends. Any time he got tickets to a game, he always thought of his friends, to see if any of them were fans of the visiting team. All these decisions came from knowing the categories into which his friends fell, but sometimes he also had to rate the value of the relationship to make the decision.

Early in the sports seasons, the games held less value for Johnny's friends. He'd think of friends he hadn't invited recently, friends who liked the visiting team, or friends who'd recently done something nice to whom he wanted to show his appreciation. He'd ask around within these categories until he found someone who was available and wanted to spend time with Johnny at the game.

As the season progressed, however, the value of each game changed. The college hockey team was always in contention for their conference championship and often in contention for a national championship. The more games they won, the closer they came to their goal and the more important the games became. Once, Johnny's dad gave him tickets to a conference championship game.

Johnny had a friend to whom he'd become close and who had done a lot for him during the years they'd known each other. They were teammates on the hockey team and best friends off the ice. Johnny appreciated the friendship they'd developed and wanted to show that appreciation. Because this game was so special and rare, Johnny felt inviting his friend would be a good way to show his appreciation for their friendship. Any regular season game would not have shown that Johnny realized and appreciated the value his friend brought to the relationship. He invited his best friend to the game and shared another positive experience that served to strengthen the relationship further.

*****

Johnny's friends in high school put in varying amounts of effort to develop friendships with him, and now, his NBFs do varying amounts to help his business. While he considers them all to be his friends, a few stand out in their contributions. Johnny wants to show these individuals how much he appreciates the efforts they've made.

Before he can rate his NBFs, though, Johnny must have some way to measure their contributions. When he was in sales, he knew, at any point in time, who gave him the lead and the status of that lead. Now, he enforces a similar tracking system with his sales force. He meets with them regularly to keep up with the status of his business and the contributions of his NBFs.

Once he has an idea of how much each individual has contributed to his business's success, based on the leads they've given him, he can rank them. Because most contributions from his NBFs are intermittent, he must revise his rankings on a regular basis. One or two of his NBFs constantly feed him new deals, but most only have access to one or two deals per year they can give. Johnny wants to let all his NBFs know he appreciates their contributions, so he gives many of them gifts in addition to the regular exchange of information. The ones at the top of the list get premium gifts to acknowledge the magnitude of service they've given him.

As a member of the hockey boosters, he often has hockey tickets to give away. His top-ranking NBFs get championship game tickets, when they are available. Johnny also has an NBF who has ties to the stadium in town. Through him, Johnny gets tickets to concerts, sporting events, and other special events that come to town. His top NBFs get VIP packages.

Johnny also uses his business to reward his top NBFs. When any of them need a product or service he provides, they get it at a deep discount or without charge, if the NBF is especially close and has made consistent contributions.

Johnny's top NBFs get the best information and the best gifts because they've given him the best information and the best deals. He doesn't reward them as a simple payback, though. His network is made up of give-and-receive relationships and is not a zero-sum game. He builds relationships by showing appropriate appreciation to those who have helped him succeed.

*****

My sales staff loves the way I do business. I go out, make connections with NBFs, and bring back the leads they will use to win new deals. They don't have to generate leads on their own; they just have to follow up on the leads I bring into the business. In return, I require they meet with me about every other week and go over the leads they're following. That way, I can track the direction of my business and the contributions of my NBFs.

Every year, I take the information I have about the contributions my NBFs have made and rank them based on the results of those contributions. In an earlier chapter, I mentioned my top NBFs sit in Coach leather chairs. This is how I determine which NBFs should receive one of those chairs. I get our courtside tickets for Denver Nuggets games through one of my NBFs and take our top NBFs out for a nice dinner and then to the game. I have NBFs, like the contractor I mentioned previously, who consistently contribute high-value leads. Because I'm in the office furniture business, these NBFs get free furniture when they upgrade or expand.

While I want to show my appreciation to the NBFs in my network who contribute to my success, I want them to think of me as much as the gift. In other words, I want them to have me in the forefront of their minds. Furniture from my inventory and experiences we share, like the Nuggets' games, are better than gifts they might enjoy alone.

For the NBFs who either didn't or couldn't contribute as much to OfficeScapes, I give tickets to Colorado Springs Sky Sox baseball games or gifts having similar value, because not all my NBFs are baseball fans. These lower-value gifts cost very little, but the impact on the relationships with my NBFs is immeasurable. Showing appreciation for even the smallest positive contributions will go a long way toward building a long-lasting NBF relationship.

RULE 22

Never tell your friends where they rank.

Johnny's friends were equally important to him, but some had a greater impact on his life than others. When he called one "friend" and another "best friend," he was merely acknowledging this fact. He wasn't saying one friend was somehow a better person than the other. His "best friend" simply shared more experiences and had more memories in common with him than the rest of his friends.

One of Johnny's teammates had been playing hockey with him since they were in the junior league together in elementary school. On the ice, they'd learned to play seamlessly and, as a result, practically tied each other every season in goals scored. This friend had been with Johnny in middle school, hanging flyers about Johnny's lost puppy and laughing when they'd found him in the back yard. He'd also been there the day Johnny received his first speeding ticket. When the local college hockey team won a national championship, they'd been at the game, together. With all of their shared interests, experiences, and memories, it was only natural for Johnny to consider this teammate his "best friend."

The only person who knew, or who needed to know, which friends Johnny considered his "best friends" was Johnny. Had he told his friends where they stood in comparison to one another, he would have created division and resentment among the friends with whom he was trying to build positive relationships. He never wrote anything down to suggest one friend might be more "important" than another might be. He kept the record of the memories and experiences they'd shared in his mind and from this collection of information, he knew who his best friends were.

*****

All Johnny's NBFs have a positive influence on his business. He doesn't consider one more important than the other, but some have shared more information and experiences with him than others. Because of these commonalities, they've contributed more to Johnny's success than the others have.

One particular NBF, like his best friend in high school, has been with Johnny since before he started his business and has gone through more with him than any of his other NBFs. Johnny originally met this NBF through the hockey boosters, and since they met, they've worked together on almost all their contracts. They consistently recommend each other to their customers, when appropriate, and this NBF has brought millions of dollars in business since they started trading information. They like going to hockey games together and found out they'd actually competed against each other in high school. This NBF has a permanent spot at the top of Johnny's list, but no one other than Johnny knows it.

Johnny doesn't want to alienate his NBFs by telling them five other NBFs in his network rank higher than they do. He doesn't even write his rankings down on paper for fear the list may accidentally fall into the hands of some unsuspecting NBF. He wants to keep positive relationships with all his NBFs and not breed resentment within his network, so he keeps his rankings in his mind and nowhere else.

*****

Trust is the most important aspect of an NBF relationship, and telling someone you appreciate their contributions, but others in your network are "better" or "more important," creates unnecessary resentment that will tear your relationships apart. Even the NBFs who are high in your rankings will wonder if you think someone else ranks higher than them or is "more important" than they are.

When I meet with my NBFs, they become the most important people in my life at that time. While they know others contribute more to my business or others receive gifts that are more valuable (they're not blind), they know they are my most important NBFs for the time I spend with them. This atmosphere is impossible if I tell my NBFs where they rank on my list because they can't trust me to keep their interests ahead of those who rank higher. It also erases any possibility of positive interaction in the relationship.

Like Johnny, I take special precautions to make sure my NBFs don't find out my ranking. It is a tool for my own use to help determine the appropriate value of gifts and information to give each of my NBFs. No one else needs to make these determinations, so no one else needs to see that information.

Summary

RULE 20: <u>Categorizing friends helps you decide who should get which information and which gifts.</u> Your friends will separate into categories based on things they have in common with you or things they have in common with one another. Use this information to make sure you are giving your NBFs what they need.

RULE 21: <u>Ranking friends helps you decide who should receive information and gifts that are more valuable.</u> When people give something of value to you, you should show your appreciation and recognize the magnitude of the contribution. Ranking your friends helps you determine how much value is appropriate for each of your friends.

RULE 22: <u>Never tell your friends where they rank.</u> Your rankings are a tool to help you build a positive relationship with each of your NBFs. Revealing the rankings to them would do just the opposite by breeding resentment within your network.

CHAPTER EIGHT

Circle the Wagons

I get by with a little help from my friends.
—John Lennon

When people work together as a team, they often accomplish more than if they were acting as a group of individuals. This phenomenon is called "synergy." Johnny saw the power of synergy for the first time when he was only ten years old, watching the 1980 Winter Olympics on TV with his dad. When the U.S. hockey team beat the Soviet team, advancing to the gold medal game, he and many others throughout the world suddenly believed in the miracle of synergy.

This band of college amateurs beating the team that had dominated international hockey the previous two decades wasn't really a miracle. A combination of good coaching and a dedication to teamwork created synergy for the team. On paper, they were deficient in every category, but on the ice, they were champions.

When Johnny saw this victory, he knew he wanted to be on a team like that. Back then, he wanted it to be a hockey team, but as he grew older, he learned synergy wasn't just something for sports. It was something that could happen within any team, whether it was his hockey team, his classmates, or a circle of his closest friends.

Synergy develops by putting the needs of the team ahead of your own. In an NBF network, this comes from the trust you've built within your relationships. You do what you can for them and trust they'll do what they can for you. The ultimate goal of your NBF team is to satisfy the customer and help the community thrive, which helps all of your businesses thrive.

Synergy requires higher goals than your bottom line or that of your NBFs. By focusing on that higher goal, everyone can be lifted higher than they ever could have been by themselves. This is where the power of a strong NBF network displays itself. When you "circle the wagons," everyone wins.

Rule 23

Always be there for your friends and
trust your friends to be there for you.

What made the 1980 U.S. Olympic men's hockey
team so special was the way they worked together so
seamlessly. As captain of his high school hockey team, Johnny
knew they would never reach that same level of performance,
but what they lacked in talent, they made up in teamwork.
Every member of the team had a position to fill and a role to
play, but everyone was ready in an instant to step in when a
teammate needed help. More important, no one was too proud
to accept help when he found himself overwhelmed.

One year, the team's goalie injured himself right
before the state tournament. The second-string goalie was only
a sophomore and had never played in a big tournament or in a
stadium as big as the state coliseum. To progress in the
tournament, the rest of the team had to step up their game and
help cover for the goalie's inexperience.

Johnny's teammates worked together just as well off
the ice as they did on the ice. Whenever someone needed a
ride, all he had to do was call one of his teammates. If a
teammate needed extra cash, someone would give it to him
without any expectation of repayment. Over the course of their

friendships, everyone had given and received equally, so no one ever felt cheated.

Teamwork was not something Johnny and his teammates did. It was something they lived. It was integral to the way they treated one another, on and off the ice.

*****

Johnny has fun in his business. Each new deal is a game for him, with his NBFs as his teammates. Winning the game is winning the contract and then giving the highest level of service to his customers. He can only accomplish this when he and his NBFs work together, back up one another, and give their collective best effort, creating a synergy that "wows" the customer and makes the whole team shine.

When a new job starts, Johnny lets each of the NBFs with whom he's working know he will be there to back them up throughout the duration of the job. If they have a problem with his company's work, they can bring it directly to him rather than going to the customer to complain. He will work with them to fix the problem before the customer ever becomes aware of it. In return, he asks they work with him to fix any problem he discovers. If they help one another, the customer will see seamless and efficient service from everyone. If they create synergy, everyone wins.

*****

This rule illustrates the strength of a good NBF network. In the Old West, when a wagon train was attacked by bandits, they would "circle the wagons." This created a defensive formation where every wagon relied on the others to protect its back. When you "circle the wagons" with your NBFs, you rely on them and they rely on you, from winning the contract to finishing the job.

Not much can hurt OfficeScapes' reputation more than a drywall contractor, painter, or others on a job complaining to the customer that we somehow damaged their work. Accidents happen from time to time on a worksite, and I'd rather have the other person be an NBF who will come to me to find a solution rather than going directly to the customer with something negative to say about me.

Contracts have timelines, and when one contractor falls behind with their portion, it affects everyone else's schedule and makes everyone look bad when the entire contract falls behind. In my business, we can't install our furniture until the flooring is in place. Once, a flooring contractor started falling behind and we were eager to get started with our installation. To keep the contract on schedule, I leant the flooring contractor some of my installers to help him get back on schedule. The customer was pleased with the flooring contractor and with us. When we step up our game and help where needed, everyone wins.

RULE 24

A strong NBF network will bring customers to you.

Even in high school, Johnny knew there were things more important than hockey. In his case, her name was Mary. He wanted to ask her out, but when he overheard her talking to the other girls about "dumb jocks with ice for brains," he knew he would need some help. He called on his friends to provide assistance.

One of his friends had a class with Mary just before practice. When class was over, he walked over to another teammate and started a conversation Mary would overhear about the upcoming practice. From time to time, he worked Johnny into the conversation in a complimentary way and looked for Mary's reaction from the corner of his eye. She already knew Johnny as an acquaintance from the chemistry study group they were in together. Combined with that knowledge, the conversations helped Mary keep a more open mind when it came to Johnny.

Another of Johnny's friends was dating one of Mary's friends. Sometimes, Johnny's friend and the two girls would get together and he would try to work Johnny's name into the conversation. After a while, Mary decided she wanted to get to know Johnny better. She knew Johnny wanted to ask her out, so she told her friend she was open to the idea and let her get the word back to Johnny. A week later, Johnny confidently asked Mary out, knowing she was going to accept.

None of this would have worked if Johnny actually fit the description Mary had for hockey players, however. Through the conversations she both had and overheard, she learned Johnny was quite intelligent and, even though he played hockey, had bigger plans for his life after college. If he hadn't lived up to the praise his friends were giving or excelled at something other than hockey, nothing his friends said or did would have helped.

*****

When Johnny hears about a new deal from his NBFs, he lets them know he's interested and asks for their help. They go to work touting his successful record and letting the new customer know about his reputation for excellence.

One NBF goes to the customer and slips Johnny's company into the conversation, adding Johnny is the best in the industry. Another makes an offhand comment, saying he assumes the customer will be using Johnny's company. Other NBFs work behind the scenes to set up a meeting between Johnny and the customer. Soon, Johnny is meeting with a new customer about a multi-million dollar deal having spent zero in marketing and advertising.

*****

We don't market with a shotgun. We market with a laser. We rarely go out looking for new customers because we have so many who continuously come looking for us. Our NBFs are constantly bringing new customers to our front door. From there, it's up to us to live up to whatever our NBFs have told them.

The clearest example of this came when a major computer company was opening a new building, and one of our NBFs got in on the project early. Throughout their interactions with the company representatives, our NBF paid attention to their furniture installation plans. They suggested the computer company look at OfficeScapes, letting them know our reputation for excellence. Ultimately, the company requested a meeting, which we gladly accepted. We didn't spend anything in marketing to get that meeting.

Our friends put their own reputations on the line to bring us into the deal. If we had delivered anything less than our best, our friends would rightfully abandon us. Their trust combined with our reputation is what lands the deal. Mary would have never dated a dumb jock, no matter what his friends said. Likewise, our customers would never do business with a mediocre company, no matter what our NBFs tell them.

RULE 25

Your friends can provide inside information to help you make critical decisions more effectively.

Johnny and Mary hit it off well, but Mary's mom didn't like the idea of her brilliant, ivy-league-bound daughter getting serious with a knuckle-dragging, soon-to-be toothless hockey player. Mary tried to convince her mom Johnny wasn't like that, but her pleas weren't enough. If Johnny was so wonderful, he'd have to prove it.

Johnny was nervous enough around Mary and was afraid he'd mess up any attempt to get along with her mom. He needed inside information in order to prepare for their first meeting. He asked Mary about her mother's likes and dislikes. He asked about how she treated other kids the first time she met them. He asked all the questions he could think to ask and then began his preparations. He wanted to have all the right answers on the tip of his tongue. He wanted to highlight his positive attributes while minimizing the ones Mary's mom was apt to see as negative. He didn't want to deceive her; he just wanted to put his best foot forward.

First, Mary's mom loved poetry, so Johnny researched her favorite poets in case she gave a pop quiz. She respected intelligence and often liked to make "dumb jocks" nervous with discussions about politics or the arts. She said they needed their egos trimmed, occasionally, and she enjoyed being the clippers. He learned not to mention hockey unless Mary's mom brought it up first and even then to get off the subject quickly. When the evening came for the first meeting, Johnny was ready.

Mary's mom was ready, too. She started out very abrasive, much to Mary's embarrassment, but Johnny's confidence couldn't be shaken. As the evening went on, she gradually became more cordial, and by the end of the evening, she was even laughing at Johnny's jokes. When Johnny left, Mary's mom shook his hand, something Mary would have never expected. The meeting seemed to go well, but Johnny wouldn't know with any certainty unless he received some more inside information.

The next day, Johnny asked Mary how she thought the evening went. Mary told him it went very well, but her mom was still uneasy because Johnny didn't talk much about his future. He didn't mention it because he was going to Boston College on a hockey scholarship. He planned to major in business, though, because he knew he'd never make it to the pros. The next time they met, he would be ready to discuss this aspect of his life in a way that would please Mary's mom.

As time went on, with Mary's help, Johnny won her over. Soon, she would hug him every time he came to the door. She was actually the first one to mention the idea of marriage to the young couple - an idea that embarrassed them greatly at the time, but eventually caught on.

*****

Johnny likes to know the outcome of a business presentation before he even steps into the room. His NBFs usually make that possible for him. The ones who are close to his customers, as well as those who've done business with them in the past, fill him in on what they expect. After the presentation, his NBFs collect feedback from the customers and pass it on so Johnny is ready for the next meeting. This cycle repeats every time Johnny meets with his customers until they become impressed with his company's ability to anticipate and meet their needs.

Johnny's reputation for customer service and satisfaction comes from knowing what the customer wants ahead of time and then delivering it. He believes customer service happens before the sale, during the job, and after the job is complete. Although sometimes he must leave things to chance, he prefers to know what to expect so he can be prepared. His NBF network helps give him the confidence to walk into a meeting knowing he will "wow" his customers. They see this confidence and this "wow" factor and know Johnny is the right man for the job.

*****

When our NBFs help us get into a deal, we always want to put our best foot forward. To do that, we like to be prepared for every meeting we have with the customer. That's where our NBFs come into play. They provide feedback from the customer we never would have been able to get otherwise. It's almost as good as reading the customer's mind. Our job with the computer company is a prime example of how this works.

Our NBFs did a fantastic job getting us the first meeting with the customer and then preparing us with what to expect. After the meeting, our NBFs came to our aid once again. The company reps liked our presentation, but thought we were a little too "pushy." It wasn't bad enough to kill the deal, so the next time we met, we deliberately backed off and watched the customer breathe a sigh of relief as they invited us back for another meeting.

Attitude isn't the only area in which our NBFs give us feedback. They also help us learn the customer's needs as far as product is concerned. When we're ready to present a product sample or demonstration to a prospective customer, we are able to give them exactly what they want because our NBFs have already told us what to expect.

In the same computer company contract, we brought out an array of product samples, including color samples, for the customer to examine. They seemed mildly impressed, and after the meeting, our NBF insider asked for their opinion. The customer had been working with our NBF for some time and had developed a better level of comfort with him, so they were frank. They didn't think we would be able to meet their needs because we didn't seem to have enough "tan" colors in our lineup. The next time we met, we placed a few blues and greens on one end of a large conference table and a few reds and yellows on the other. In the vast expanse between these two, we placed nothing less than every variation of "tan" we could find. The customer was visibly shocked to see so much tan and remarked that maybe we did have the colors they wanted, after all.

Every customer is like a boyfriend or girlfriend's mother you are trying to impress. You only get one shot, and if you blow it, it's hard to work your way back into their good graces. Going at it alone is taking a shot in the dark. You need your NBFs on the inside to feed you information about the customer, which you can then use to make a perfect presentation the first time. If you do somehow put the customer off, you need your NBFs to give you feedback so you can correct the error immediately.

Summary

RULE 23: <u>Always be there for your friends and trust your friends to be there for you.</u> By helping one another, the customer gets superior service and no one gets a bad reputation.

RULE 24: <u>A strong NBF network will bring customers to you.</u> As long as you maintain a reputation for excellence, your NBFs recommendations will be your biggest marketing tool, saving you time and money.

RULE 25: <u>Your friends can provide inside information to help you make critical decisions more effectively.</u> With a strong NBF network, you never have to go into a meeting blind and unprepared. Let them give you the inside information and use that information to "wow" the customer. This "wow" factor will help you achieve market dominance.

CHAPTER NINE

Practice Makes Perfect

*Theory may raise your hopes but
practice raises your income.*
—Unattributed

Applying many of the NBF rules requires face-to-face interaction with each of your NBFs. The best times to build these relationships and lay down boundaries to which you expect your NBFs to adhere is at breakfast, coffee, or lunch. The best places to meet are quiet enough for casual conversation where you must sit at a table and order from a menu *(Rule 10)*. This even applies when you go out for coffee. While Starbucks and other similar local or national coffee houses are popular and provide a wide variety of coffee drinks, a small diner is much better for NBF meetings. Places where you order from the counter prevent you talking to your NBF until you're seated, and then your time is limited, not to mention these restaurants tend to have a much higher noise level. Buffets are also a poor choice because you can't hold your NBF's attention. You want your NBF focused on and thinking about you and the conversation, not the dessert bar. At buffets, you both must get up and leave the conversation to get your next serving, so conversation becomes fragmented *(Rule 13)*.

Many national chain restaurants would meet these requirements, but to be memorable, you should find some place in your city that is special or unique *(Rule 16)*. If your NBF is higher on the food chain *(Rule 21)*, this meeting may be the only thing of value you have to offer, especially in the early stages of your networking efforts *(Rule 11)*. Here in Colorado Springs, I have several such places to choose from scattered across town. In the historical part of town, Old Colorado City, and in nearby Manitou Springs, many small, family-owned cafes offer unique fare in a quiet, relaxing atmosphere. The Broadmoor, a five-star luxury hotel with world-class chefs and top-notch service, also has a variety of restaurants and bars available to the public. Most people don't make it a habit of going to these restaurants, so each of these options would qualify as a memorable treat.

For me, the El Paso Club is the best venue for meeting my NBFs. The El Paso club is a historic, members-only club for gentlemen established in 1877 by a group of the city's founders. The building housing the club was once the residence of Prof. James H. Kerr from my alma mater. The founders wanted this club to attract only the best of society's gentlemen and enacted several policies to ensure they met this goal. For example, they banned both firearms and "intoxicants" from the premises, discouraging those who were not true gentlemen.

The aura of high society still exists, and the building has remained practically unchanged through the years. The opportunity to see the exquisite architecture and the rare art collection makes just entering the club a treat by itself. The quality of the food and the chance to bump into local business leaders or politicians only adds to the thrill my NBFs get by being invited there for lunch. Some NBFs I've invited to the club numerous times still get the same thrill each time they come. One, in particular, I nicknamed "Senator" because of the way she works the room, greeting people and being "seen."

A typical day starts with a breakfast meeting with an NBF at 7:30 AM *(Rule 15)*. Afterward, I email any leads I've obtained to my sales staff and myself from my Blackberry and send a quick text to the NBF I will be meeting for lunch *(Rule 14)*. I confirm the place and time and mention I am looking forward to the meeting. I make it to my 9:00 AM business meeting, which could be a meeting with a customer to look over samples, a meeting with my sales staff to go over leads, or any other of the day-to-day duties of running a business *(Rules 2, 3)*. I leave work in time to make it to the El Paso Club a little before 11:45 AM *(Rule 15)*.

When I enter the club, the host always greets me as "Mr. Husak." Personally, I think it's worth the membership dues just for that kind of service, especially when meeting NBFs for the first time. If my NBF is already there, I shake his hand and greet him. If not, I wait and greet him when he enters the reception room. The staff members know where I prefer to sit, and one of them shows us to the table, still addressing me as "Mr. Husak."

The table is slightly removed from the rest of the dining area. Even though the room is already quieter than almost all the other restaurants in town, this location is isolated so we can focus on each other for the duration of the meal *(Rule 22)*. It also makes it easier for my NBFs to open up and speak more freely if they know they won't be overheard *(Rule 10)*. As soon as we are seated, I start asking my NBF about his family, hobbies, and other things related to his personal life *(Rules 4, 13).*

When the waiter arrives, he brings a Diet Coke and a glass of peanuts for me and a menu for my guest. Because I come here often, the staff members know my preferences and bring things out without having to be asked. I also know the specials and the menu so well I don't need to see one *(Rule 15).* This allows me to remain focused on my NBF.

After my NBF orders, I go right back into the discussion I was having about his or her personal life. The waiter may come to fill a water glass during this time, but he does not constantly ask whether we need anything. When he does come to the table, he knows I prefer to keep up the conversation with my NBF and does whatever he needs to do quickly and quietly.

I transition into our discussion about business once my NBF receives whatever he's ordered and I have my Cobb salad, with no bleu cheese, and a bowl of green chili *(Rules 13, 15).* While we're eating, we go over the information we wish to share. I have a few leads already picked out that should have value to this NBF, and I'm ready to hand them over *(Rules 11, 12, 20, 21).* This discussion may take quite a bit of time, especially if my NBF begins raving about the food. I've had NBFs who wouldn't order anything more than a side salad at any other restaurant order an appetizer, salad, entrée, dessert, and coffee, and finish it all, when I treat them to the El Paso Club.

The waiter does not bring a check to the table when we are done with the meal, and this is another reason I prefer the El Paso Club. The club does not allow guests to pay. Instead, they automatically put the bill onto my account, so we have no awkward moments while the check is in the middle of the table and each person wonders if the other person will pick it up. I believe if I get one good lead from the meeting, then the lunch pays for itself in the profits from the resulting contract, so I don't mind picking up the tab. Besides, it's just another effective way to give something valuable to my NBFs *(Rule 12)*.

As we leave the building, I give my NBF a tour so they have an opportunity to take in the beauty of the architecture and the artwork *(Rule 9)*. It also gives him the additional opportunity to greet others and to be "seen," like my "Senator." At the same time, I am wrapping up any loose ends from our business discussion.

After my NBF departs, I get to work with my Blackberry. I start by emailing any notes or leads I received from my NBF to myself, so I can remember them, and to my sales staff, so they can get to work on them, immediately.

Next, I send any details I promised to my NBF from lunch, with either an email or a phone call to his voice mail. This kind of immediate response lets your NBFs know you care about them and about their success. It also works to strengthen your relationship with him or her *(Rule 3)*. Once I've taken care of that NBF, I think about the information I've just received and think about any other NBFs who might find it useful. I don't reveal my source *(Rule 17)* and I keep the "spill rule" in mind *(Rule 19)*, but if I have information I can share, I send it immediately to the NBFs I believe to be in the best position to use it *(Rules 16, 18, 20, 21)*. These "Scooby snacks" go a long way toward building trust with your NBFs. They are accustomed to people who give and take. Giving something like this, without expecting anything in return, will set you apart from the others in a very good way *(Rules 6, 7, 8)*.

I also check my Blackberry for anyone having a birthday, anniversary, or similar life event on that day. I call them and wish them well for whatever the occasion may be. Calling is much more personal than email, so for these types of personal celebrations, I prefer to call so I can say, sing, or even yodel my wishes to them *(Rule 9)*.

After that, it's back to business *(Rule 2, 3)*. I make my 1:30 PM meeting and, when I get a chance, I schedule more meetings with more NBFs to start the cycle, again *(Rule 4)*.

CHAPTER TEN

Market Dominance

*Don't aim for success if you want it;
just do what you love and believe in,
and it will come naturally.*
—David Frost

In most networking guides, the general theory is you obtain quality through quantity. The idea is to play the law of averages in order to build your network. They suggest if you meet enough people, you will eventually find someone who can help your business. One guide instructs you to "Plant a lot of seeds" to build your network. To them, success is building the largest network possible without regard to quality of each individual connection.

With an NBF network, members have something to offer because you chose them specifically for what they have, not for what they may have or who they may know. That's why I believe larger networking and leads groups are so ineffective in the long term. A lot of time and effort goes into these groups with only a chance you will get anything of value. Your NBFs will always have something of value. You spend your time and effort cultivating strong relationships you know will be beneficial rather than sifting through a pile of contacts who may or may not have anything to offer.

The differences between the conventional networking strategy and the NBF networking strategy lead you to a new way of thinking about success. To get the most out of your NBF network, you must redefine what you believe about successful networking results. When you have a network focused on quality rather than quantity, the rules of success change drastically.

Success Rule 1

*The amount of information you
receive is not the primary
measure of success.*

The quantity of the information you receive isn't a good measure of networking success. With NBFs, the strength of your relationships is the best way to determine the success of your network. In a traditional network, you may receive a lot of information that has very little value, much as it was with the leads group that gave me only two valuable leads over 14 years.

Even when a contact gives you quality information, it only leads to short-term gain if that person never gives you anything else or becomes disinterested. Only through strong, long-term relationships can you achieve the success OfficeScapes has seen.

Remember, you should always expect to give more than you receive, so the information you trade with your NBFs must be less important than the relationship you share. Successful relationships make up a successful network and lead to success in business.

Success Rule 2

*A successful business should be
fun to operate.*

This rule is a natural extension of Success Rule 1.
When you focus on the relationships you have within your
network, rather than what others have to offer, it's easy to
relax and have fun. When you're constantly wondering when
the people in your network will give you the next juicy bit of
information or getting angry because they haven't already
done so, you can't have fun. If, on the other hand, you trust
your NBFs to bring you information when they have it
available, you can have fun. This doesn't mean you focus on
the relationship to the exclusion of your business. You must
blur the boundaries between business and pleasure. Doing
business with a bunch of random contacts will become tedious,
but doing business with a team of best friends will be fun and
successful.

SUCCESS RULE 3

*If you walk away from a meeting or leads
group with one lead you didn't have
before, then you're successful.*

Many networking guides put pressure on you to get as
many leads or contacts as possible, or at least get some preset
number. This takes the fun out of socializing, meeting new
people, building relationships, and doing business. Success
Rule 2 tells you business should be fun, so things are a little
different in an NBF network. You go into one of these events
looking for specific people in specific industries who can help
your business. Once you find someone who fits that category,
you can speak to them at length and begin to develop a
relationship rather than collecting some contact information
and moving on to the next person and repeating the process.
The person you spoke to at length is more likely to remember
you than the person to whom you introduced yourself to get #4
or #5 in the number of contacts you needed to be "successful."

SUCCESS RULE 4

If you have one email or voicemail per day with a referral, you are successful.

This comes from making yourself memorable to your NBFs. It starts with meeting them and spending time getting to know them, as mentioned in Success Rule 3. Keeping yourself in the forefront of their minds takes effort throughout the relationship. At OfficeScapes, we do this in two ways. First, when we get new leads we think our NBFs can use, we get the information to them immediately. Second, when we give freebies to our NBFs, we're careful to make sure the NBF won't forget the source of the gift. I've told you our top five sit in Coach leather chairs and when a newer, better model comes out, we replace it and take the old one back. Every time the owners of those chairs come into their offices and sit down, they automatically think "OfficeScapes." We don't give freebies away to our NBFs that will take their minds off us or make them forget us, even momentarily. If we were to give an NBF a trip to Vegas, for example, what they will remember is how much fun they had in Vegas–not that OfficeScapes made it possible.

SUCCESS RULE 5

You are working toward the
"silver-platter" deal.

These are the deals your NBFs bring to your front
door, pre-assembled, gift-wrapped, and served on a silver
platter. They are the holy grail of networking and the reason
you built your NBF network in the first place. While your
competitors are waiting for some glimmer of a new deal,
you've already signed the contract and begun work.

Knowing about a job before your competition gives
you a tremendous advantage, and not just because you get the
deal before they do. When you approach a deal before the
customer puts the contract out for bid, you are in a position to
negotiate the terms of the contract rather than making cuts to
be the lowest bidder. When a contract goes out for bid, you are
limited in what you can do for both your business and the
customer. When you negotiate a contract, you have more
flexibility. You can maximize your margins while
simultaneously providing the customer exactly what they want
and need. OfficeScapes' largest profits have come from silver-
platter deals, but we were always fair to the customer. By
negotiating the contract, the customer received the highest
level of customer service and the right furniture for their

needs. Their level of satisfaction increased, as did OfficeScapes' reputation.

SUCCESS RULE 6

When your advertising and marketing budget approaches zero, you are successful.

With a strong NBF network, you have very little need to advertise. All of your business will come from your NBFs. Some will be silver-platter deals, while others will be leads you have to investigate and chase down on your own. All of this happens without TV or radio spots, newspaper ads, mass mailings, or any conventional method of attracting business. These methods work for the products you buy at department stores or discount stores, but not for OfficeScapes and not for you.

I like to say we market with a laser, not a shotgun. With our NBF network, we can identify a potential customer and get them interested enough in OfficeScapes to request a meeting, or at least accept our request, without spending a single penny in marketing and advertising. With the shotgun approach, we'd blast our message out into the public and hope one or two of the pellets make contact.

Another way to think of it is we fish with a fly rod, not a net. The fly rod is our NBF network bringing a specific deal to us, while the net is a conventional approach, hoping the deal you want gets trapped inside.

Businesses do not become successful on hope. They become successful on profits. The lower your advertising budget gets, the less you are relying on hope and the more successful you'll become.

SUCCESS RULE 7

You are successful when you have left a legacy or a mark on something and brought it to a higher level.

Jim Maguire owns the Overhead Door Company of Colorado Springs. He has a lot of fun, and his interactions with the community lead to more relationships, which leads to more business success, which leads right back to having more fun. I look at Jim Maguire as a model for business success, especially in a smaller market. He leads a full life and enjoys participating in community events such as the local 4th of July parade. When I said, earlier in the book, that business should be fun, I was thinking of Jim Maguire.

The impact Jim has had on his company and the people who work for him is rivaled only by the impact he has had on the community. He "is" Overhead Door *of Colorado Springs*. Moving anywhere else would never work for him because, through his network, he has become an integral part of the community, with deep roots that hold him firmly in place.

While I don't claim to have the type of influence and impact Jim does, I'd like to believe I am well on my way. In 2007, the Chamber of Commerce in Colorado Springs selected me as the "Small Business Person of the Year." In 2010, I received the International Association of Administrative Professionals (IAAP) Executive of the Year Award. In the various write-ups that went into the IAAP award, one theme stood out and was put succinctly in the nomination letter. "…OfficeScapes IS Peter."

I see this statement, not as a compliment, but as a challenge and a responsibility. I believe the purpose of my business is to harness the gifts of people in order to let them shine. Every individual has a unique set of gifts and abilities, and it's my job to recognize those abilities and put those people in the right positions so they can thrive. I enjoy placing people in the right positions and then just sitting back and watching them glow as they do what they do best. If I'm not positively affecting a person's life, I'm not doing my job properly and cannot succeed.

Jim Maguire continues to influence so many people and is so deeply rooted he is stuck, geographically. The upside to this is he has a large ring of protection. While it would take him ten years or more to recreate the relationships he currently has, it would take others in the community even longer to adjust if he went away. For this reason, people in the business and political arenas are willing to do a lot to keep Jim happy.

I recently experienced this phenomenon when I went to the bank for a business loan in a time when banks were more reluctant to lend money. I gave my presentation and the bank came back with their offer, which wasn't what I needed. When I suggested this loan package may not be suitable for my needs and maybe I should "shop around," the loan officer went back to put together a new offer. This time, it had all the features for which I'd originally asked and suited our needs perfectly. The turnaround stunned me, and I asked the loan officer about it once we'd finalized the deal. He replied, "You're one guy in this community I don't want to piss off." Again, this stunned me, so I asked why he didn't want to piss me off. He said, "You know more people than anybody I know, and I didn't want to piss you off." My network became my protection.

At the end of the day, we're trying to have an impact on our community. By putting my customers, my employees, my network, and the rest of the community ahead of me and by showing genuine love to all of them, a small office furniture supplier can—and will—make a difference.

Made in the USA
Las Vegas, NV
17 February 2022